T0349024

Don't Go Back to Sleep

Get going! You only have twenty-four hours…
and remember, so does everyone else.

P A U L   E   C A L A R C O ,   J R .

BALBOA.PRESS
A DIVISION OF HAY HOUSE

Balboa Press books may be ordered through booksellers or by contacting:

Balboa Press
A Division of Hay House
1663 Liberty Drive
Bloomington, IN 47403
www.balboapress.com
844-682-1282

Because of the dynamic nature of the Internet, any web addresses or links contained in this book may have changed since publication and may no longer be valid. The views expressed in this work are solely those of the author and do not necessarily reflect the views of the publisher, and the publisher hereby disclaims any responsibility for them.

The author of this book does not dispense medical advice or prescribe the use of any technique as a form of treatment for physical, emotional, or medical problems without the advice of a physician, either directly or indirectly. The intent of the author is only to offer information of a general nature to help you in your quest for emotional and spiritual well-being. In the event you use any of the information in this book for yourself, which is your constitutional right, the author and the publisher assume no responsibility for your actions.

Any people depicted in stock imagery provided by Getty Images are models, and such images are being used for illustrative purposes only.
Certain stock imagery © Getty Images.

Cover Art: Rachid Kallamni
Spiral Image: Kim van de Sande
Evolution Chapter Title Art: John Hampshire

Scripture quotations marked KJV are from the Holy Bible, King James Version (Authorized Version). First published in 1611. Quoted from the KJV Classic Reference Bible, Copyright © 1983 by The Zondervan Corporation.

Scripture quotations marked NKJV are taken from the New King James Version. Copyright © 1982 by Thomas Nelson, Inc. Used by permission. All rights reserved.

Scripture quotations marked NIV are taken from the Holy Bible, New International Version®. NIV®. Copyright © 1973, 1978, 1984 by International Bible Society. Used by permission of Zondervan. All rights reserved. [Biblica]

Print information available on the last page.

ISBN: 979-8-7652-4498-2 (sc)
ISBN: 979-8-7652-4499-9 (hc)
ISBN: 979-8-7652-4994-9 (e)

Library of Congress Control Number: 2024902096

Balboa Press rev. date: 10/30/2024

Dedicated to Noah James Paul and Mason Matthew

"But do you want to know, O foolish man,
that faith without works is dead?"
James 2:20 NKJV

"If you abide in Me, and MY words abide in you,
you will ask what you desire,
and it shall be done for you"
John 15:7 NKJV

CONTENTS

INTRODUCTION

Success is not a secret system, nothing written here has not been said before, every motivational speaker that I have crossed in my experience have already asserted everything that I have compiled here in this book; each one is but a synthesized compilation of previous paths of past knowledge and then each adds their own special spice to the recipe.

I cannot discount the fact that there is indeed value to the motivational speaker game and a phenomenal rush of insight is always gained when attending a mega seminar. However, like any teacher, like this book, they are simply a channel to present the material that is meant to bring out the best in you. What they provide you with is the spark, but it is you that has to do the work to bring out your greatest potential. Spoiler alert, the true secret is: only you know what that is.

The same can be said with the guru. YOU are the guru and the guru is but a conduit to connect you to your inner you. In this life, you are here as both a student and a teacher. In this very moment writing these words to you, I am merely a student whom has over time amassed a sizeable knowledge base. In the context of an author, I might be seen as a teacher but I am a continuous student of life that is always open to receive, always continuing to learn, always continuing to grow, and always continuing to create.

It is imperative that you are ready to move forward with your life in a new, more productive manner. Many people mistake a busy day for a productive one. You need to laser focus your attention towards productivity not just movement in circles but forward. Coaches all agree that the person has to be one-hundred percent dedicated to their goals and all-in. I firmly believe when we truly decide, it is then that the road of life rises to meet us. A brilliant metaphor for success is the iceberg. When you see the successful out there in the world, all you see is the outcome, the grand finale, the tip of the iceberg. What you do not see is the lifetime of work, the preparation, the failure(s), the suffering, the agony, the persistence, the doubts, the risks, the sacrifices and the endless trials faced by that individual to get to the pinnacle of their field. You are only seeing the end of the movie and do not realize the horrors that some of the protagonists had to endure to reach their place of prominence. How much rejection could you endure on the path to your dreams? Oprah Winfrey was given leave from her position on Baltimore's WJZ-TV's news team because she was considered unfit for television and she was in her words: devastated. No success story is devoid of trials and challenges. To be triumphant in any endeavor, you have to get to the essence of your-self. To accomplish this, you have to establish firm, deep and authentic roots to build your future.

A most challenging yet necessary precursor to taking the most solid first step towards your dreams is to embrace forgiveness. Now you may be thinking, how the heck does forgiveness relate to my goals? As you will learn, success is awarded to the authentic, not solely the hard-working. If everyone with fantastic resumes got the position then there would be no such thing in the corporate world called: middle management. It is the brightest stars whom are seen, and if you want to get recognized, then you must not only work hard but you must get to the essence of your-self. Believe it or not, this process involves forgiving yourself that that past could have been any different than it is, and that this moment could have been any different than it is right now. Once you accept that the present moment is a product of what was, and what is, IS in your control RIGHT NOW now and you have the ability to not be held hostage by the ghosts of your past. What you have is the right now and every moment hereafter to create the future that you desire. Remember, life does not happen to you, it happens for you. All you have been through has value, all you are is all you need and the key is locking in the on target, moving forward with focus, determination and some gusto.

Vincent Van Gogh stated: I dream my painting and I paint my dream. It is time to let it all go and to get on with your best life. You are only limited by your imagination, desire and the sky's the limit.

The title of this book was inspired by the prose of the eleventh century poet, philosopher and mystic Jalal ad-Din Muhammad Rumi; commonly known as Rumi.

> The breeze at dawn has secrets to tell you.
> Don't go back to sleep.
>
> You must ask for what you really want.
> Don't go back to sleep.
>
> People are going back and forth
> across the doorsill
> where the two worlds touch.
>
> The door is round and open.
> Don't go back to sleep.

We will return to these words at the end of the book, my hope is at that point they hold deeper meaning to you. Many times, I have witnessed the whispering of the sunrise, many times I have been privy to the messages in the breeze at dawn and many times I have been jolted by divine inspiration while the world was still sleeping.

Moreover, before you begin anew on your journey inward and outward, I wish for you to know that you will have moments where you feel completely alone. Do not worry, alone is not just a feeling that exists when you are by yourself. I have felt alone in large rooms that were full of people, I have felt alone with my own family, I have felt alone lying next to my lover and I have felt alone by myself. You may be feeling that way right now, but know you are not alone in your feelings and know you are never truly alone. The ultimate goal is to find whole-ness, one-ness and security in your own company. Respectively, it took me many years to fully appreciate the serenity in being alone.

"Be alone, that is the secret of invention; be alone, that is when ideas are born."

Nikola Tesla

Solitude is imperative to creativity and is immeasurably valuable to you. Once you find the solace and grace in your alone time, you will unlock the essential keys on the path to your goals. Clarity in your head and especially in the heart are the places where all truth, knowledge and wisdom flow. Only when you are able to clear the static of the outside world will you truly know who you are, will you truly know your feelings and will you know your true desires. The brilliant German scholar Johann Wolfgang Von Goethe succinctly posited:

"Talent is nurtured in solitude. A creation of importance can only be produced when its author isolates himself, it is a child of solitude."

Listen up and understand the consequences before you get started. Put the book down if you are not ready to be honest with your-self. It is only you that will be able to peel back the layers. It is only you that is responsible for you. It is only you that will need to push through the tired. It is only you that is responsible to read the books, write the papers, budget your money, get the degrees, apply for the jobs and to put in the work. Our contemporary social narratives have been rewritten, our cultural expectations have shifted and our general collective work ethic has diminished profoundly in these last few decades. We presently reside in an immediate gratification laden, fast food expectation and Social Media Millionaire culture. I have personally observed a shift in the past twenty-five years in both teaching and parenting that most people desire the outcome but do not wish to fully engage the process. Antithetically, if you ask the winningest coaches in the business what makes the best player, they will all agree that it is their focused unrelenting work ethic. You have to be willing to put in the hours and push above and beyond until you reach your goals. What people desire is the tip of the iceberg and are not willing to do what was required below the surface that positioned that individual to manifest their blessings.

START LATE. START OVER. START SCARED. START AGAIN. JUST START!

The quickest and simplest way to success is to start. You cannot learn to drive in a parked car. A boat can never reach its destination without leaving the port. While you are reading this book, you will recognize that there is a tremendous significance to THE PROCESS. The goal of this book is to not only inspire you but to assist you to get to a baseline and build a strong foundation. Nothing you have been through, nothing you have learned, nothing you have experienced is ever a WASTE of time except time WASTED. Most importantly, I wish to help you understand, handle and above all sustain your future success.

THE WHAT

"Be anxious for nothing, but in everything by prayer and supplication, with thanksgiving, let your requests be made known to God"

Philippians 4:6 NKJV

Let us begin as we do in a yoga practice. Let us ground ourselves in the moment. Let us find our center and begin with intention. Take a moment to breathe deeply and remove all of your attention to anything but the immediate surroundings; begin to clear the space and clear the clutter in your mind. Find your breath, take several deep breaths and settle into your-self. Let the thoughts come. Let the thoughts go. Let the thoughts flow. Life is ready to teach and to reveal its lesson but you must first find the silence. You have to take time amidst your busy day to put your phone away, even better, get out into the loveliest peaceful spot in nature so you may find serenity. The most important part is to find a place to be alone in blessed solitude that is <u>not</u> your residence. Make time for quiet moments. The world is loud and inspiration always whispers.

> **"We need time to defuse, to contemplate. Just as in sleep our brains relax and give us dreams, so at some time in the day we need to disconnect, reconnect, and look around us."**
>
> **Laurie Colwin**

1

Once you have found a place and a state of being where your breath is even and your mind begins to ease, then gently ask yourself these several questions:

- What is it that you want to do?
- What are you interested in?
- What is it that the voice in your head says that you desire?
- What do you imagine yourself accomplishing?
- What are your goals?

What you need to find is the fountain of potential in your life. What you have to do is learn to be comfortable alone. Most people do not want to be alone. Most people feel an immense need to be around people. Yes, we are social creatures and I too enjoy the company of my people. However, you cannot think amidst the noise of others. You have to unplug from it all and it will be uncomfortable at first. You cannot think amidst the noise of the world. You cannot think amidst the scrolling and streaming media. You cannot get to your essence of being amidst the buzz of this industrial environment. What you need is to be alone to delve into deep, quiet contemplation. You need to be alone to reach the core of what you want. You need to be alone to get to the core of your inner being. Seclusion is a price you will pay on the path to success. The process and practice of being in the wilderness alone is designed to allow you to see what is really important. Consider this: the teacher is always silent during the examination. It is in this dark desolation that you will begin to face who you are and it is only in this quiet will you be able to realize your true calling.

> **"If you want to be happy, set a goal that commands your thoughts, liberates your energy and inspires your hopes."**
>
> **Andrew Carnegie**

Goals? What are your goals in life? What do you want out of life? These are tough questions for many people. Goals are directly associated with our happiness in many ways both giving us purpose and motivation.

2

Several success gurus have similarly posited that our daily life is subject to change but that goals are what pull us forward regardless of any-thing that can happen to us.

We all have things we want in our life. We all have things we desire in our heart. We think that once we have them we will be happy. Interestingly, you do not experience joy achieving a goal. Joy is actually attached to setting a goal and the progress towards it. In our culture, we are taught the opposite, which is why we are consistently disappointed. We learn to associate our wants and desires with the material world, though the logic is eternally flawed and we will never ever be satisfied because our desires are consistently expanding into infinity.

When we have a goal, when we set a goal, we are placing ourselves upon a path to achieve that goal. A want may waver, a desire may shift but a true goal when decided upon with our full heart then becomes part of our destiny. True goals are not accomplished simply in the decision. True goals are achieved in their deliberate decision, deliberate focus, deliberate planning, deliberate action and deliberate dedication.

Goals are attained by deciding to continue over and over, again and again, every single day irrespective of any outcomes or challenges until you reach your destination. It is never about what you are capable of... it is about WHAT YOU ARE WILLING TO DO. However, let us not get too far ahead of ourselves. Let us get you firmly grounded not just in your breath but your complete being. Let us get your goals so firmly established that your plans will not crumble because you have them built upon a solid foundation. We don't plan to fail but typically we falter because we fail to plan.

> **"First, think. Second, believe. Third, dream. Finally, dare."**
>
> **Walt Disney**

WHAT is it that you **WISH** to achieve? What is it that will ignite the fire in you? What is it that will inspire you? What is it that will get you up when you get knocked down? I use goal, wish and dream interchangeably; they are synonyms to me. I am someone who believes in the power of prayer. I am someone who believes in miracles. I urge you to be extremely mindful and clear exactly what it is that you request into the ether. Life has a way of granting our wishes and you need to be very detailed, deliberate and definite of that which you wish. In my experience, many people find themselves unhappy in situations that they actually WANTED and many people find themselves unhappy with the things they so very much DESIRED. We can do our best to avoid these circumstances by spending quality time with ourselves in solitude and doing the necessary work to reach our heart's true essence. Seek and you shall find. The answers you seek never arrive when the mind is busy, they arise when the mind is still.

Clarity. It is time to be super clear on your objectives.

What is it that you want to achieve? What are your interests?

WHAT DO YOU REALLY WANT?

What compels you? What moves you? What is calling you?

What are your talents? What are your gifts?

Clarity is POWER. It is said that knowledge is power, this is true, but it is the powerful that know how to strategically navigate the world. Dale Carnegie once said: "Knowledge isn't power until it is applied." The powerfully wise are able to use their knowledge to intelligently filter information in order to maximize their outcomes. You must understand that knowledge makes some arrogant but true wisdom always humbles and the truly wise are silent.

If you cannot answer the question: WHAT DO I WANT? Perhaps you may already HAVE IT or you now need to get on the path TO IT. The words on these pages are my call for you to take action or perhaps this book will serve as a series of affirmations that you are on the right path.

YOU HAVE TO GET SPECIFIC to GET to YOUR DREAMS. Why is it that you have trouble being specific? Are you being intentionally vague because you do not want to be held accountable? Do you have anxiety around commitment? Is there an internal fear of getting what you really want? Do you have negative beliefs about what you can accomplish or possess? I want you to USE this book, it is YOUR book so WRITE in the margins, get different colored pens and a highlighter and GET READY to GET GOING!!! GET READY to GET STARTED towards your calling. No more taking easy way out. No more comfort zone. No more settling. No more accepting less than you are worth. Limbo is the only bar that should be set low in life. Are you satisfied with mediocre or do you want miracles? It is time to go above and beyond the ordinary and build an extra-ordinary life.

KNOW WHAT YOU WANT to your CORE!

What are the things that you get excited about when you wake up in the morning? What are the things that give you a boost of energy when you think about them? What are the things that spark your interest and creativity? It is in your passions you will ultimately find your purpose.

So…let's garner clarity by examining this very moment.

Start with WHAT ARE YOU HAPPY ABOUT RIGHT NOW? What are you genuinely happy about in your life and world right now?

Next WHAT ARE YOU NOT HAPPY ABOUT RIGHT NOW? What are you truly unhappy about in your life and world right now?

"A Goal is a Dream with a Deadline."

Napoleon Hill

In my profession teaching undergraduate students, I present them with these questions and commonly most students do not know exactly what they "want" to do. A few "think" they "know" where they will be in five, ten, fifteen years. For most, it is not about exactly what they want, it is more a vague lifestyle preference that they are considering when thinking about their endgame view. It is incredibly important to put your life in perspective and plan for the future now. If you want to succeed and attain your goals, you have to write them down. Get your journal and start writing what you want. Be specific: I earn, I own, I drive, I live, I work, I have, I am…

General Goals/Desires
Short Range Goals
Long Range Goals

Your responses to the above are not set in stone, the wisdom of time has illustrated to me that if you were to be asked again the very same questions in the future they will likely shift and they will as you evolve to your highest self. You should be flexible as you move towards your goals, your goals usually do not look exactly as you might imagine; most often they are even more grand than you expected. What you think might bring you happiness and joy will change over time once you develop a deeper understanding of life and how you define happiness. Happiness is an intriguing concept we will explore later as it has an infinite variety of interpretations and definitions depending on the individual, the direction of our focus and what we value in life.

> **"The man who starts first gets the oyster; the second man gets the shell"**
>
> **Andrew Carnegie**

Get a journal and begin to write more, think more, muse more about what you want to achieve. It is important to start this process as soon as possible. Continuously review the items that you write, set deadlines for each item, make a list of what you need to do to accomplish those tasks, and organize it into a check-list. You now have a place to begin and a tangible general action plan. Periodically return to your journal to assess the progress you are making towards your goal, check off your accomplishments and add more items to the list. It is imperative to remember to keep the path to your goals fluid and that you will constantly shape, reshape and sharpen your focus as you move into the FUTURE.

"Victorious warriors win first and then go to war, while defeated warriors go to war first and then seek to win."

Sun Tzu

Always expect to reach your goal, but it will not happen on its own, you MUST prepare to reach your goal and BE READY because when the opportunities are presented to you, will you be in the position to accept them? It is better to be prepared for an opportunity and not have one, than to have an opportunity and NOT BE PREPARED. Preparation will always increase your chances of success.

BE READY, to be ready, to be ready, to be ready, to be ready.

Reflecting on my life, there were always windows of opportunity presented and you have to BE READY to seize the moment. Most often I did but there are more than several instances that I recall that my procrastination and shortsightedness taught me the most valuable lessons. What stories are you telling yourself that are hindering your progress? I am not a morning person? I have time? What time you wake up is not a personality type! Your waking hour will be determined by your goals! **The What** will determine your alarm in the morning. **The What** will determine who you spend your precious time with. **The What** will determine your work ethic. **The What** will not let you sleep until you have completed the task(s).

You MUST be ready or you may miss the moment
…then you have to wait until the next
window, if there is a <u>next</u> window.

Do you have a vision for your life? Begin to appreciate the things you have that you are happy with right now. Find the silver linings in each moment of every day and this will help you get on the fast track that will lead you to your dreams. It is easy to get scattered and lose focus once you start to manifest and rise. You have to understand that this is a continuous process of revision, sharpening, refocusing, and reorienting. There are no ceilings in this life as you will learn. The ceilings will become the next floor.

Is money your goal? What will you "do" to make that money? What will you do when you earn that money? Do you have a definition of life? Have you considered fulfillment in your definition?

Let's get started!

"Begin, be bold and venture to be wise."

Horace

Try to not think about all of it at once. All you can do is what you can do. All you can do is to begin. The purpose of this book is to help calibrate your compass and to set your course towards your goals. All you can do is to consistently move forward and step-by-step check the items off of your to-do list. HOW is not the question. How is never any of your business. Decide on what you want to achieve and you are that much closer to having it.

Aim high and miss
DO NOT AIM LOW and HIT!!!!

What are you going to do?!!! Are you willing to do what is necessary? Are you willing to push through the challenges? You and only you can decide the answer. You must decide: "I am going to make it". Repeat this very simple mantra EVERYDAY:

Yes, I can
Yes, I will

The most difficult hurdle to overcome is to remain steadfast in the pursuit of your goals. The purpose of this book is to help you find the inner-will and vigilance to commit and succeed; to look up instead of looking down and believe that you can have anything you desire.

THE WHY

"He who has a why to live for can bear almost any how."

Friedrich Nietzsche

What is your why? Before you can address this question, you have to evaluate exactly where you stand in relation to everything you desire. I am sure you did not think there would be this much preliminary work but one of my trite phrases (I often tire my children with to their chagrin):

Do you want to do it the right way or the hard way?

Let's begin with an inventory and personal assessment to find out your exact location. Similar to the GPS, you must pinpoint where you stand in relationship to where you would like to go, in order to figure out how you are going to arrive at your desired destination.

The reasons come first and the answers come second.

What does that even mean? Consider the question: What is your "why"? You need to seek further into the depths of your being and find your reasons why you get up every day. Let's start right here and write in your journal the things that motivate you, the people that motivate you, and the reasons why you want what you want. I know it is a challenge to get to your core but as you make your way through the book and move onward and upward, you will return to these writings.

WHY?

…because as you begin to address the reasons, more answers will arise. It is a part of the constant and reflexive process discussed earlier, which is WHY it is important to return, check in and see if there is consistency or a need for revision. Perhaps there are things to add, subtract, modify and / or sharpen with more detail as you move closer towards your goals. For example, I look back at my vaguely scattered goals from my youth into my twenties, every single one ultimately manifested by the time I was forty-five. In all honesty, there is not one single goal that I had for this glorious life that did not find its way to fruition. The question I then started asking myself, now being at the pinnacle of my career and life: Why did I not dream bigger?! What if I had dreamed bigger?! What do I do now?!

Sociologically, we set our expectations based on our lived experience and reference groups. While I am incredibly happy in all that I have become and beyond content with the life I created, I also know if I had been even more focused, had even more of an imagination and had I read this book… I might have accelerated my growth and success. The Japanese have a word: IKIGAI or purpose, which has been proven to enhance both happiness and longevity. My purpose is continuously evolving to remain in an inspired state of being. AND that is the underlying reason WHY I was led to write this book. My why evolved into a wish to inspire others to achieve their goals. My goal is to provide you with the tools to unlock your greatest potential and achieve your DREAM LIFE.

"No wise man ever wished to be younger."

Jonathan Swift

I am asked the question periodically: would you go back and change anything if you could? The answer is always: no. I would not want to lose the retrospective wisdom I have acquired in my years of life. Nor would I want to re-live those most challenging, difficult and painful times over again. Most importantly, I would not change one experience because it would completely change the overall outcomes; The Butterfly Effect. Life is not easy and it will never be devoid of complications and suffering. Life is the classroom and you are its student.

What motivates you? Who motivates you? What is your driving force? Who is your driving force? Who are the people you call when both good and bad things happen to you? What matters? Who matters? What matters most? Who matters most? Who might you acknowledge at the podium when receiving an award or accolade? Your why is going to give you the advantage. Your why is going to give you the inspiration.

Continue thinking and write in your journal as you delve deeper into the driving force(s) underlying the goal(s) you have for life. As well, journal about: Why are you interested in these goals? Why are these goals important to you? Who will you share your accomplishments with? Who will you be when you get to the finish line?

> **"What you get by achieving your goals is not as important as what you become by achieving your goals."**
>
> **Henry David Thoreau**

Close your eyes and consider what an amazing life is to you. Describe that in as much detail as you can in your journal. Now for the uncomfortable question: Why are you not there yet? Why do you not have that amazing life you are describing? Why are you not living the life you desire?

Why is all this WHY thinking important? Your why is going to give you the push. Your why is not just going to get you out of bed in the morning; it is your WHY that will get you up before your alarm clock. It is your WHY that truly drives you. It is your WHY that will help you push through the challenges that plague your path. Motivation will only get you going but it is your why that will KEEP you going. Why can be your biggest adversaries serve as your personal accountability coach; you decide.

"Where your fear is, there is your task."

Carl Jung

Are you uncomfortable making a change?
Do you fear failing?
Do you fear loss?
Do you fear the unknown?
Why?
Do you fear the monsters under the bed?

Life presents an interesting set of mental challenges to overcome as you work to build your best life. While you are doing things that are beneficial for you, you will simultaneously experience the opposite. When you are learning something new, you will feel unwise <u>but</u> you are becoming smarter. When you are working out, you will feel weak <u>but</u> you are becoming stronger. When you are saving money, you will feel broke <u>but</u> you are amassing wealth. When you dig and unearth your past trauma, you will feel broken <u>but</u> it is actually healing those wounds. When you set boundaries with people and the world, you will feel lonely <u>but</u> you are positioning yourself for real people and true love to enter your life. To truly achieve success you will be matched by your willingness to face the discomfort and overcome those opposite feelings. Write your fears down in your journal so you can finally meet them face-to-face. You need to acknowledge your foes if you wish to conquer them in battle. Know thy enemy. Take this fight seriously, it is the fight for your future.

"There are 1,000 lessons in defeat but only one in victory."

Confucius

Do you know what failure feels like? Have you tasted the dirt in your teeth? Have you been at rock-bottom? We are conditioned beings and it might be your experiential history that is inhibiting you from fully engaging and committing to the present moment. You have to move past "the past". You have to engage and face fully the present reality. You have to push, you have to face the mirror, you have to take the tests wholeheartedly, as uncomfortable as they may be; it is the only way to break-through to your goals.

Think less and Trust more.
Why are you here?

Have you considered the ontological notion of the purpose of your existence? Whatever your faith or belief system might be, I am sure you have spent time with the question of why. Why are you here? What is the purpose of your birth? All religions collectively press us to not just seek faith in a higher power but to work towards a union to that source/inner-being/GOD within ourselves. The Sioux, a North American indigenous tribe has a saying: The longest journey you will make in your life is from your head to your heart. In this book there are tools to assist your travel across this expansive eighteen-inch road to discover the essence of your being. True success is a union between the physical and the spiritual worlds. True success is attained when you win both externally and internally the treasures of this life. I believe this is why you will commonly find the wealthiest people of the world are constantly seeking more in the material without satisfaction, as the truth is to satiate the non-material desires within. Conversely, if you travel to the poorest nations in the world, you will find their populations are happy despite the desperation. Prayer, meditation, yoga and martial arts at their core help you to reduce the dissonance in the mind, so then you can focus and tune into the heart; tune into your inner guide.

Who is your why?

Consider the people that are the most important in your life. Consider the people who made sacrifices for you to be here. Do this right now, in this very moment, while reading this book write down those names in your journal. Consider the people who have been your cheering squad since the beginning. Consider those ancestors who came before, paving the way for you to be where you are, putting you in the position to take these next steps towards greatness.

In American culture we tend not to consider our lineage as do the indigenous populations. We need to acknowledge those whom were here before us and consider those ancestors who paved the way, sacrificed and prayed for you to be here. Take some time to consider "all" of those divine paths that merged to bring you into being and brought you to this very moment. No one accomplishes anything completely on their own, there is a bit of a myth to the self-made success story. Success is never a solitary process.

Is there someone you are getting up at four thirty am for? Who WILL you NOW be getting up before sunrise for after your journaling? Who motivates you? Who are you motivated by? What do they mean to you? What contributions have they made to your life? How can you now return the favor?

Give the people who invest in you a return on their investment. Give the people who support you something tangible. Honor your family, consider if your name is on something, even as small as an email, you should have some sense of personal pride, responsibility, integrity and honor. To have and to hold a reverence for the past will foster an increased intrinsic drive on your path. Viktor Frankel said: **"A man is pushed by drives but pulled by values"**. There is a need to assess what is indeed driving you. You will find life is a path towards self-realization. If you do not know that already, today begins your awareness. Along with your consciousness, you must learn to take advantage of every opportunity to being you closer to your goals. A motivational hack is to use external declarations of intent that you assert to *your* people: mentors, colleagues and family. These expressions of intent and your goal(s) will serve to invigorate your commitment to your tasks as you will now have an increased sense of accountability. As well, you will have their support when you might need it along the way. Do not deny assistance on the path.

"Success without honor is an unseasoned dish; it will satisfy your hunger but it won't taste good."

Joe Paterno

Let's look at this from another angle, consider the word: can't. You need to begin to remove that word from your vocabulary. How often do you use the word? What is your relationship with the word?

Say the words: I can't. How does it make you feel?

It is so very important to figure out your reasons why. Once you find your why, not only will the answers will begin to flow but your motivation will then shift into relentless overdrive. Once you can find those focus points, your convictions and determination will help you push through anything that comes in your path.

You must make failure unacceptable.
Failure must not be an option.

Why? …because you have to keep your promises to yourself. If your why is strong enough, then you will prevail despite fear and failure. Nothing in your way will be able to stop you if you are truly driven towards your goal.

"Your talent determines what you can do. Your motivation determines how much you are willing to do. Your attitude determines how well you do."

Lou Holtz

I always consider this fact before I endeavor anything: One hundred percent of attempts **not** made FAIL. Are you willing to show up? Most people just show up in life? When I say, are you willing to show up, I mean are you willing to put your entire self into the process. The successful all say that you have to make the moves, you have to take the shot; you have to fully commit.

I failed, is much more meaningful than:

What if?

"It is said that before entering the sea a river trembles with fear. She looks back at the path she has traveled, from the peaks of the mountains, the long winding road crossing forests and villages. And in front of her, she sees an ocean so vast, that to enter there seems nothing more than to disappear forever. But there is no other way. The river cannot go back. Nobody can go back. To go back is impossible in existence. The river needs to take the risk of entering the ocean because only then will fear disappear, because that's where the river will know it's not about disappearing into the ocean, but of becoming the ocean."

Khalin Gibran

Be a warrior not a worrier. The person you want to be is beyond where you are now. We may encounter defeats but we must not be defeated. Our success may lay on the other side of that battle and we cannot consider what will happen but stay focused on where we want to be and move onward. Worry is like a rocking chair, it gets you nowhere. Worry is the anticipation of the negative. When you increase your FAITH you simultaneously decrease your worry. In addition to winning the battle with fear, the foremost reason people succeed is persistence. The sting of defeat may activate your passion and boost your drive. You must consider your passion level, you have to deeply desire your goal because without passion and desire you will surely not give your all and likely give up. If you do not feel a burning desire in your heart for your goals, if you do not feel fired up every day, this is an indicator that you need to adjust your focus. It is not enough to simply have a gift, you have to have passion. If you are focused on your goals, you will know that the trajectory is more important than your present position. Nothing else will matter.

> **"The secret of genius is to carry the spirit of the child into old age, which means never losing your enthusiasm."**
>
> **Aldous Huxley**

Passion is a major success x-factor. You cannot purchase or pretend passion, you either have it or you do not. It is an innate drive; it comes from within and it is displayed outwardly. Though invisible and intangible it is of infinite value because it does matter profoundly. Passion is similar to what is said about love, you either love someone or you do not; there is no in between. Passion is the fuel that drives you. You should not need a cheerleader to inspire you. There should be no excuse that can get in the way of your goal. You should wake up every morning with an unrelenting spirit to grow and be your best YOU. Be your own hype-man. A true commitment, means to do what is necessary whether you like it or NOT. Do not compromise your future with anything less than one-hundred percent focus. Find and pursue your goals with passion and conscious consistent effort. If you do not love the pursuit to your core, you will not achieve it. It is irrationally difficult and most people fall short because they do not have the endurance to push through the finish line.

> **"Expose yourself to your deepest fear; after that, fear has no power, and the fear of freedom shrinks and vanishes. You are free."**
>
> **Jim Morrison**

The greatest enemy of progress is fear. Doubt is fear's first cousin and is very convincing to limit your efforts and thwart your progress. You must use your power to shift your perspective; as fear will steal your future if you allow it.

FEAR: What if?
FAITH: Even if!

The key is to just begin and know that faith and fear go hand in hand. Fear and doubt will be ever present but you need to refuse to be intimidated by it. You will always have to push through something to get where you are going. Be cautious and careful but do not be frozen by fear. You can give up and accept the present circumstance or work until you overcome it and conquer the trial and persevere; and if you do not make the attempt, you will <u>never</u> know. If you do not try, you will <u>NEVER</u> KNOW WHAT YOU ARE CAPABLE OF. The most common reason that people don't start is typically based on false beliefs. It will never work. I can't do it. I'll never get through this. I can't get over this. I can't get out of here. Begin the shift towards: How can I do this? The majority of people fail because they fail to start. Morgan Freeman said two very simple yet profound things in an interview:

"BULLSHIT…everybody can…the key to life is COURAGE …the bus runs EVERYDAY"

Begin to change your definitions and perspective of what you are able to accomplish. You have a choice. You are choosing not to get out of bed. You are choosing not to work out. You are choosing not to read. You are choosing not to study. You are choosing not to _____. You must believe that you are a powerful creator of your reality. You must believe that you have a choice! Every day you must choose to push through fear positively; it is imperative to your success. How do you see obstacles? How do you see fear?

- o Forget Everything and Run
- o False Expectations Appearing Real
- o False Expectations About Reality
- o Future Events Appearing Real
- o Failure Expected and Received

The successful thrive by transmuting the negative thoughts by turning them into fuel. It does not mean that your courage will not waiver. You will have moments in the battle that you question whether or not you will survive; that is NORMAL. The key is to maintain your mission's course despite each step being shadowed with darkness AND to have the courage moving forward though fear is whispering doubt into your ears.

> **"I learned that courage was not the absence of fear, but the triumph over it. The brave man is not he who does not feel afraid, but he who conquers that fear."**
>
> **Nelson Mandela**

Use fear to your advantage and rejoice even more in your triumph. What if? What if you win? What if you can have it all.? Say it: **What if I win.** I mean it, say it again out loud and feel the feeling. **What if I can have it all.**

- o Face Everything and Rise
- o For Everything a Reason
- o Feeling Excited and Ready

Recognize this FACT: Faith and Fear are exactly the SAME, with both your belief is based on what you cannot SEE. Faith is the belief in advance for what will make perfect sense in reverse. You are not born a winner. You are not born a loser. You are born a chooser. I would much rather walk in FAITH, knowing from experience that I not only will be able to manifest my desires and dreams. Fear does nothing positive for you but derail you from the path to your blessings. Faith is your key to manage and overcome the highs and especially the lows of life. Fear and Faith are a choice and you can only choose ONE! You must believe that you are worthy and deserve to be on the journey. If we do not believe we can accomplish something, we have already failed. We must step up and make the attempt with our whole hearts.

> **"Circumstances make man, not man circumstances."**
>
> **Mark Twain**

Doubt is a pointless waste of time. You put one foot in front of the other with hope and your best is all you can ask of yourself. Failure is often the entry fee to success. Failure can simply be avoided by consistently moving forward and not sitting still; the rolling stone does not gather moss. Never give up. If you do fail, trust in the failure, see amidst the struggle your victory and that it is now time to rise and be the hero of YOUR story. Rise up to meet your potential. Rise up and exceed your limitations. Rise up beyond your imagination. To reach the apex you will have to LEARN how to FAIL and continue onward.

"Live your life as an Exclamation rather than an Explanation"

Isaac Newton

Every winner has a collection of losses but they were the prerequisite to their victory. The average person will run from the challenge, make excuses and take the easy way out. As the maxim states easy come, easy go. Remember this logic, if you do what is easy, life will be much more difficult. It takes work and dedication to get to where you wish to go, nothing worth anything in this world worth anything was had easily.

"Don't wish it was easier, wish you were better."

Jim Rohn

You will learn to rise, face yourself in the mirror, fight the good fight and you will fail FORWARD every time. If you get knocked down, you MUST get up! Get back UP! The successful always do one more. The successful athlete always does one more repetition. The successful telemarketer makes one more phone call. The successful influencer makes one more post. The successful entrepreneur starts one more business. The successful applicant sends out one more application. The successful will all tell you that their breakthroughs all came through the philosophy of going just that little bit extra beyond where they thought they could; just one more. One more repetition. One more book. One more seminar. One more phone call. One more investment. One more course. One more try.

"Life is getting up one more time than you've been knocked down."

John Wayne

Here are some points that by the end of this book you will over-stand and be able to apply in your life.

- You must know that failure is NOT death
- Change the language of your goal
- NEVER is it a failure but a lesson, a blessed chance to revisit your goal
- Failing may get you to your TRUE GOAL
- Find the grace to understand as you continue onward
- Adapt to adversity
- Fail and move on and make it bigger and better
- This new unknown will be the stronger foundation of tomorrow
- You must Move on, get UP and get after IT

AND, THE MOST important facet and vintage adage on failure to commit to memory: IF YOU FAIL TO PLAN, PREPARE TO FAIL.

Many failures can be avoided through appropriate planning and foresight. If you do fail and there isn't anyone that does not at some point fall short, you must know that there is strength in failure. The strength you gain in your redirection will be what secures your stability in your success. There is wisdom acquired in the process on the journey to your destiny.

"Don't judge your greatness by your shadow at sunset."

Pythagoras

While you are down, stay there just a few moments and take inventory of everything in your life. It may feel like the lowest point in your life. In my experience, if I try and fail, I do not consider it a loss; there is always a lesson. Every time I did not get what I wanted, it led me to some-thing greater. Embrace the opportunity. Embrace the freedom.

Embrace the uncertainty. Embrace the lesson. What is there to learn? Think deeply about how you are going to move forward with greater intentionality. Never is failure a setback, it is always a setup.

I love reflecting back on my life and the journey. Robert Fulghum wrote a very influential book with a very powerful title: All I Really Need to Know I Learned in Kindergarten. Life and its secrets to an abundant life are so simple. You may not agree but there is even science to prove that you learn faster when you are PLAYING. However, we reach adulthood and we learn to over-complicate life. Take time to recall those simple and free times of your youth. Take time to consider the philosophies that you heard and sang so joyfully as a child. Ironically, the secret of success is to get back to that simplicity of mind. Once we do, we realize at some point we lost our truest selves and our dreams along the way.

Row, row, row your boat, gently down the stream,
merrily, merrily, merrily, merrily, life is but a dream.
Use your imagination, be creative, think outside the box.
If at first you don't succeed try, try again!
Take naps.
Success is not elusive but you need to do the work.
You are important.

The kindergarten method is one that inspires you to follow a creative cycle that begins with imagination, creation, playing, sharing, reflecting and then a spiraling back again full-circle to the imagination. In short, you need to find balance between the serious and playful in the pursuit of your goals.

"What one man calls God, another calls the laws of physics."

Nikola Tesla

Robert Fulghum stated: "It doesn't matter what you say you believe – it only matters what you do". This book is intended to take you on a journey through a variety of postulates and respective techniques. Take what you need, take what inspires you, run with it and discard the rest. I wrote this book primarily to fulfill a vision from the year 2015 that grew in its intention to reach both my students and in particular my son MASON to illustrate that I do indeed practice what I preach. As Tesla asserts above, we all have different perspectives on how the world operates and devoid of those specialized understandings, the world still revolves and the sun will rise and set every day. Success can be a simple three-part, non-sectarian pursuit as well. *though the author believes that faith gives you the special-sauce on your burger.

Vision, follow-through and consistency:

- Get in the right frame of mind
- Find a point to focus on what is in your control
- Take your vision
- Strategize and plan
- Execute that blueprint every single day
- You need to be open to alternate plans, ideas and solutions

You do not always win. There are lists of undefeated athletes and sports teams, but the most impressive story is the collegiate wrestler Cael Sanderson. Cael went undefeated during his four-year NCAA career winning 159 matches. In high school, he did actually lose three of his 130 total matches and during a red-shirt year before he began officially on the roster at Iowa State. If you think about it, he had more to lose as he progressed along his flawless career. Every time he stepped onto the mat; he stood the chance to be dethroned. The lesson for us is to master the ability to navigate the ebb and flow of life, to learn to ride the current and to get back on the mat after a fall.

Any book on success would be remiss to not mention professional basketball's number twenty-three. The iconic Michael Jordan's most impressive and under-reported statistic is that he missed nine-thousand shots. During his career, Michael Jordan missed game winning shots. Michael Jordan's team, while number twenty-three was on the floor lost close to three-hundred games. However, Michael Jordan is still regarded as one of the greatest players in this history of the game. Why? He was relentless in his pursuit of his passion and dream. He pushed HIMSELF beyond the boundaries of the game itself. He was quoted saying:

"Some people want it to happen, some people wish it would happen, others make it happen."

Michael in a conversation with Tony Robbins relayed that he demands more of himself than anybody else could possibly expect of him. He asserted that he does not compete with other people. His primary goal was to push beyond what he was capable of every single day. It is such a simple formula: pursue and do your absolute best and you will achieve your absolute best results. Pursue unceasingly personal excellence, knowing beyond that everything else is out of your control. Oprah Winfrey once said: **"excellence is the best deterrent to racism or sexism." Be excellent in all endeavors. People notice and remember.** What most people do not do, is push themselves to their absolute limits. Coaches in every sport will tell you, there is an x-factor beyond the physical and that is TENACITY. Others may be better on paper but the best-of-the-best have an unrelenting drive to succeed. You are not here to prove yourself to others. Instead, it is you versus you. You are here to prove to yourself that you are worthy. As the self-help guru Louise Hay urges us to say every day: I approve of myself.

"I can bear any pain as long as it has meaning."

Haruki Murakami

Suffering is inevitable during our lifetime and the beliefs we associate with our existence is our decision. We all will suffer but it is what you do despite the suffering that makes the difference in the outcome of your life. During a phase in my life, I experienced a personal loss like no other. My entire world was imploding in on me and an internal agony that was utterly unbearable. However, I did not let that stop me from getting up early in the morning. I did not let that stop me from going to work every day. I did not let that stop me from serving my community.

It was during those five months of pure pain that I produced more than several significant lines on my resume and experienced a profound shift and up leveling in my life. While spending the majority of my days grieving, I was serving as a positive influence in the lives of those around me. One day, that weight lifted and I had made it through the storm. Remember this, there is no trial that lasts forever.

What we need to constantly remind ourselves, since there will always be pain, the pain associated with stagnation is worse than the pain of movement. The pain of failure does not hurt as much as the pain of regret because the former has led you closer to your goal. The pain of trying again does imply the potential to fail again but it is on that path to your goals that brings meaning to your existence. Trying again means risking again. Trying again means believing again. Trying again means hoping again and you cannot lose hope. When we lose hope, we die a thousand deaths. The younger you are, the more chances you have, the bigger risks you are able to take, the larger sacrifices you are able to make; so, make them. Risk while you have the luxury of time. Find and don't lose that hope. Find your Polestar and keep on your path to your dreams. The worst pain in life is the regret of not trying. The worst tragedy in life is wasted time and talent. These lessons you do not and will not realize until it is too late. Pain only lasts for a season, the joy will last for a lifetime.

"You need imagination in order to imagine a future that doesn't exist."

Azar Nafisi

Use your imagination and learn to be open, be creative, be resourceful. Bruce Lee said: Be water. Allow me to expand: Be a wet sponge. You need to not only be able to go with the flow, but you have to also be ravenous in your desire to learn. Consistently seek ways to break through to the next level. I have found that often times, the way things ultimately worked out were not exactly how I planned, expected or anticipated. Periodically squeeze out the sponge, discard what doesn't serve you and begin anew towards what is meant for you. Sometimes this squeezing is not your choice. However, in my experience it was through this involuntary process along with God's grace I was able to achieve even larger and more magnificent achievements than I had originally anticipated. The key to success is to maintain firm desires and a flexibility to be open every day to the path that is <u>yours</u> and <u>allow</u> the road to <u>rise to meet you</u>.

> **"The writer must have a good imagination to begin with, but the imagination has to be muscular, which means it must be exercised in a disciplined way, day in and day out, by writing, failing, succeeding and revising."**
>
> **Stephen King**

Take a moment right now to think about your dream life. Take some time and use your journal to review your previous lists and add more detail to your vision. Stop and really imagine it, really feel it. You have the power to make all of that happen. You have to use your creativity and break free from your present patterns to get to the new places you wish to go. Remember that everything in this world was once a vision that some "one" brought to fruition. Look around, in your hand or on your electronic device is this very book that was once a mere spark of inspiration in my imagination.

My hope is that you will dig deeper into you. My hope is that you will dig deeper into the depths of your imagination. **Be an archaeologist of your soul.** My hope is that you will create fantastic things that are beyond your own expectations. As Andy Warhol said: Don't think about making art, just get it done. CREATE, then let everyone else decide if it's good or bad, whether they love it or hate it. While they are deciding, keep going, keep creating and make even more art. Always take the energy you have and put it into something that moves you closer to your goals. We will delve deeper into the power of your imagination and the tools necessary to make your dream life possible later in the book. **Start now!**

THE WHO

"To be yourself in a world that is constantly trying to make you something else is the greatest accomplishment."

Ralph Waldo Emerson

Do you have more ideas now of whom it is that you want to be? Do you know who you are? Take a few minutes to really think about who you are. In this moment, write some adjectives that describe who you are. Now look at those words and think about how they make you feel.

Are you presently a wandering generality? I want you to be a **meaningful specific**! You cannot get to your highest self and dreams without specificity of intention. Who are you now? Do you know who you are? What do you think when you think about yourself? Do you love your self? Robert Nesta Marley said: Open your eyes, look within. Are you satisfied with the life you're living?

Look at yourself
Look at yourself in the mirror
Do you like what you see?
Are you who you wish to be?
Are you proud of yourself?
Are you happy?

Are you satisfied?

Shakespeare penned the essence of this existential search for our identity in the play Hamlet. He encapsulated it in these powerful notions through the advice from a father to his son.

> **"This above all: to thine own self be true, And it must follow, as the night the day, Thou canst not then be false to any man."**

As we move through the world, do we walk in our own shoes fully? Do you walk completely in truth? Is there a conflict between who you are and who you want to be? <u>THIS IS YOUR WAKE-UP CALL</u> to begin to consider who you are. <u>THIS IS THE TIME</u> to take your self and your time seriously.

> **"The only person with whom you have to compare ourselves, is that you in the past. And the only person better you should be, this is who you are now."**
>
> **Sigmund Freud**

Through the discovery of who you are, you will be able to solidify your purpose and destiny. Consider your goals but now let's start to think deeper about the connection it has to your identity. Begin to journal about the skills you would like to add to your resume. How do these skills align with your inner being? Begin to consider seriously who you would like to be, it is through this new knowledge that will ultimately shape your identity and your life.

Educational
Career
Personal
Family
Lifestyle
Hobbies

There are so many facets of what makes us who we are and we should be deliberate creators in the development of our identity. You must believe that you can be who you wish to be but there is a cost. You will have to trade in your old ways, places and activities to make room to develop the new version of you.

"You can never be overdressed or overeducated."

Oscar Wilde

THE WHERE

Once you realize the who you are <u>now</u>, then you may consider who you will be. It is time to calibrate the GPS with your location so it can determine the directions for the journey. Once you see yourself for who you are. Once you exorcise and illuminate the deepest darkest parts of yourself. Once you accept the NOW and what WAS is <u>no longer</u>. You will then begin to align and then be able to realize your greatest potential. Once you completely believe in the power within you. Once you completely believe you can have what you desire. It is then what you desire will be yours. Every day you have to take the leap of faith and claim the crown that yours. You are royalty. Say it out-loud: I AM ROYALTY.

> **"If a man knows not to which port he sails, no wind is favorable."**
>
> **Seneca**

You have begun the process to determine where you wish to go. Now it is time to evaluate where you are. Where are you RIGHT NOW?

Where you are right now possesses tremendous value. Life coaches all shout the mantra: focus on the goal, focus on the destination, focus on your desires. Of course, it is imperative to know our deepest desires. We too have to know exactly where we stand. We have to honestly assess our current limitations so we may be able to build. We have to establish roots so our best future may thrive. You cannot go anywhere until you surrender to where you are at. As stated earlier, we have to know where we ARE because we have to prepare to LEAVE this place. Surrendering to the present moment, past failures and even those that may occur in the future is NEVER about defeat. To surrender is the ability to move forward and open yourself to new possibilities. It also means that you must relinquish control and the ability to embrace the unknown. There is no imaginable way that you can get to the life of your dreams without knowing its relationship to your present location; you cannot set your destination and get directions from a GPS system without a current location. Be fully in this moment and create space for the unexpected and extraordinary opportunities and miracles that await you. AGAIN, you cannot get to where you desire to be without leaving behind where you are.

"A wise man changes his mind, a fool never will."

Spanish proverb

At any moment you can choose to change your entire life, it is up to you. You decide WHO YOU ARE in this world. You decide WHERE you want to go in this world. You are the captain BUT you must learn to SAIL. You are not a prisoner to the definitions anyone has given to you up to this point in your existence. Consider the captain of a sailboat, they are constantly adjusting according to the wind; that is how you should consider your approach to life. Look around you, look at your surroundings. Do you like what you see? Are you where you wish to be? Are you proud of where you are? Do you see clutter? Is this a healthy environment to enhance your growth? It does not matter <u>where</u> you are right now. As long as you are fully aware of the limitations of your present port location, you may then make the necessary adjustments to your compass toward the place of prosperity.

Even a bountiful garden can grow on the rooftops in the middle of a metropolis. Take time to evaluate what things around you need attention at this very moment? Take a serious look at your living space. As you look around, begin to take control of your life and consider if you are living and emulating the best version of yourself. Get your journal and write what you see right now? Write about your present reality. Write about what is and where you are in this moment. Now, look beyond where you are and expand your perspective. What do you want? What do you want to change? Where do you want to be? Where do you want to go? You must find clarity in your desires. In order to receive the gift, you must make your request known. Ask and it shall be given.

FAITH

Do you wish to enhance your life circumstance? Do you wish to enhance your lived experience? Do you know what it takes to get to the life of your dreams? FAITH. Are you starting to believe it? Are you starting to see it? Henry Ward Beecher said "The soul without imagination is what an observatory would be without a telescope." Can you really imagine it being you? Do you have faith that what you want is on its way? Do you believe in miracles? The power of faith and belief are the keys to the blessings that are waiting for you beyond your doubt. You can believe everything is a miracle or you can believe that miracles do not exist. You choose! I believe, if you can hold it in your mind, you can hold it in your hand. If you can imagine it, it will be true. Believe that you have received your desire and your desire will be yours. Thoughts are things and what you feel you attract and what you imagine you will become; your future begins in your mind.

> **"Now faith is the substance of things hoped for, the evidence of things not seen."**
>
> **Hebrews 11:1 NKJV**

Faith and honesty are affiliates and they are your teammates to get you on the path to your goals. However, you must address the following questions and until you can answer with a resounding "yes" to all of them there is absolutely no way you can rise to your greatest potential.

- Can you be vulnerable?
- Can you be honest with yourself?
- Can you sit with yourself?
- Are you able to be alone in solitude?
- Are you in good company with yourself?

It is in your vulnerability you will find your armor and greatest strength in the world. It takes true courage to be REAL in this present world. Authenticity is the most courageous endeavor and we are consistently bombarded with ideas of who we should be, what we should do, how we should live and so on. My final nudge to write this book was watching my sons struggle to build their identity in this digital age. More than any other time in history, we are inundated with constant images everywhere, there is virtually no escape from the programming screens. Literally, we are presented with three options: copycat, artificial intelligence or authenticity. No matter where you are, you are plugged in and we have to be mindful as we traverse the path of self-realization. To children, adolescents and young adults it is problematic as they are building their identity amidst ceaseless buzzing and subliminal suggestions of insecurity, desire and needs. I am thankful to have experienced the world pre-Internet as the media was limited by both its design and technology. We had to go out of our way to get to media. We had to go home or to the office to get our messages. In these times of information whiplash, we need to learn to unplug and ground ourselves periodically in what is REAL.

> **"Most people are other people. Their thoughts are someone else's opinions, their lives a mimicry, their passions a quotation"**
>
> **Oscar Wilde**

Authenticity is the most important line on your resume. Authenticity is the only filter you should use on social media. You need to stop wasting your time playing a role. You need to stop wasting your time trying to be some-thing. You need to start maximizing your time being you, doing you. You can be an imitator out there in public.

You can be dishonest in the company of others. You can be deceitful and you <u>will</u> find success. However, when you return home, you will have to sit in your house of cards. As Bob Marley said: you can fool some people some of the time but you can't fool all the people all of the time. If you build a life on false pretenses, like a house on a poor foundation, it one day will eventually collapse. A related adage: if you are always honest, you never have to remember what you previously said, ever. Moreover, the best and the brightest shine from within. If you cannot be real with yourself, I guarantee, anything your do, anything you present will be received as disingenuous and you will not prosper long term. Life is a marathon not a sprint. Success is about maintaining endurance through all of what comes your way until you get to your goals.

Science has recently proven that authenticity is the most powerful of human emotions. In a study using the Scale of Positive and Negative Experience, also known as the SPANE scale, researchers were able to quantify the frequency of positive and negative affect between people. They found that authenticity is four-thousand times more powerful than love. While there are critics of the test and I am not an expert in the field, and though I still BELIEVE in the SUPREME POWER OF LOVE, there is something to be said to have science highlighting that being your true self in body, mind and spirit should be your ultimate goal. In musing the relationship between love and authenticity, it makes sense for love to come second. If you put forth your most authentic self, it allows for your most authentic love to flow forth and attract your most compatible people into your life. Moreover, research has shown that people who live more authentic lives tend to be more positive, happier, have higher self-esteem and better relationships.

No one can ever beat you at being YOU! Choose every day to show up as <u>you</u>. Make the conscious choice every single day to allow your truest inner soul to shine brightly. I always consider with humility, though I can at any time be replaced at my job, there is also not another person on this planet that is exactly like me that can do it like <u>me</u>. I am special,

I am unique and I know on a soul level that no one can deliver the same service I can, in the same way, ever.

Take the time to consider deeply the following questions:

- What is it that you think about yourself when you are by yourself?
- Do you compare yourself to others?
- Do you value YOU?
- Do you see and love YOU?
- Do you share the real you with the world?
- Are you comfortable in your own skin?

As you delve deeper into who you are, another caveat to self-realization is deconstructing your own self-perception(s). Do you hold yourself in high regard? Are you confident? Do you see yourself as capable? We must constantly and consistently acknowledge and embrace a sense of self-worth because everywhere we turn, we are told we are not enough. Even within your social circles there may be people that tell you that you are less than whole, you are ineffective, you are incomplete and you are not good enough. It is time for you to break the programming and break free from limiting messages, people and beliefs.

You must believe to your core that: **YOU ARE ENOUGH!** If you experience these feelings, you must immediately shift your thoughts and focus; thoughts are optional. You can have a thought but never let the thought have you. I have found it takes about thirty seconds to accomplish a redirection. Under these circumstances, I suggest the using following mantra: I am enough. I am whole. I am loved. I am worthy of endless blessings. No-thing is out of my league. Take deep breaths and internalize those words of TRUTH.

You must change the way you look at yourself. Appreciate that for everything that you cannot do, there are many things you "can" do. You have so many gifts, talents and abilities that you have yet to discover. If there are objectives that you desire to accomplish, start today and think about what can you do today that will move you towards the who you wish to be.

What you can do immediately, right now, today:

- Grab your journal and create a to-do list
- Listen to a podcast / lecture
- Meditate
- Read a book
- Create / Build / Imagine
- Engage a physical activity you enjoy

> **"What is the fruit of these teachings? Only the most beautiful and proper harvest of the truly educated— tranquility, fearlessness, and freedom. We should not trust the masses who say only the free can be educated, but rather the lovers of wisdom who say that only the educated are free."**
>
> **Epictetus**

Nothing that you invest your time in is ever wasted time. No skills that you acquire will ever be useless. As I remind my students, education will never close doors for you. Your skills and degrees can only open doors but it is you that has to do the knocking. Any efforts and investments in yourself that you make will ultimately pay dividends either directly or indirectly in your life. Any investments that you make in other people, will also return to you in spectacularly unexpected ways.

> **"A flower does not think of competing to the flower next to it. It just blooms."**
>
> **Zen Shin**

Who you are is not what you do. The who you are is what is deep inside of you. The who you are is what you think about when you awake in the middle of the night. The who you are is what are you doing when no one is looking. <u>The who you are is what you dream about</u>. You need to find the "who" you truly are, and it then you will begin to become the who you dream to be. Only then you rise to who you are destined to be. What limits have you placed on yourself? What subconscious restrictions may be hindering growth? What invisible chains are inhibiting your greatest potential?

THE ELEPHANT

A young boy was walking by a large elephant at the circus and was perplexed that this massive creature was secured by a small rope. He decided to ask the trainer why the elephant did not need chains or cages to secure him, knowing he was capable of upending the entire tent, and even overturning motor vehicles if he desired. The trainer replied: "What we do is secure the elephant with a rope tightly when they are young and small. We keep them tied on a short rope at a time when they are <u>not capable</u> of escape. Even when they fight, they cannot break free, so over time they simply stop struggling and no longer attempt to get away. The funny part is, we do not change the size of the rope for the adults because they believe it is the rope that binds them to the fence, ha-ha-ha-ha-ha". The boy shook his head in amazement that these powerful creatures could be taught submissiveness and all those years be held in bondage by that same rope from their childhood. If only they knew...

The story is greater than the characters, it reminds us to acknowledge the power of conditioning. As a sociologist, this is where we find a merging of my discipline with our sibling psychology. There is a complex nature or shall I say nurture of the human psyche. There is a depth to the subconscious that is addressed by psychoanalysts like Sigmund Freud that link much of our adult experiences / desires / ways / outcomes to that of our childhood. The key is to dig deep and recognize what are you holding on to or what rope is holding on to you? Carl Jung stated: until you make the subconscious conscious, it will direct your life and you will call it fate. What limits have been imposed on you systemically, culturally, educationally, religiously, socially? When did you stop believing in yourself? When did you stop believing in miracles? When did you stop believing in your dreams? Wherever you are YOU are NOT stuck. You CAN go wherever you want. You CAN do whatever you want. You CAN do anything you WISH. The rope of your youth can bind you no longer.

> **"Start by doing what's necessary; then do what's possible; and suddenly you are doing the impossible."**
>
> **St. Francis of Assisi (attributed but not proven)**

If you are reading these words then second, third and fourth chances are still available to you. If you are reading this book, you must know that each time you miss an opportunity, you will have to work harder to get back on track. It is NEVER impossible. Nothing is impossible. Keep reading! Even if it seems it is, stay the course, stay convicted to your path and realize that you are a powerful GIANT KILLER. David only had rocks and a slingshot but he also had courage and faith. You must know in your bones that you are stronger than your worries, fears and doubts. You need to *shake it off* like Taylor Swift those self-limiting beliefs conditioned by your socio-cultural and lived experience. You can never be too late, what you need to do is begin to SHOW UP. Start showing up for YOU. You need to stand in faith and confidence against everything you THINK you know right now. If you are not present you cannot receive your gifts. Most people are not willing to build the physical, mental and emotional confidence that is necessary to get to where they want to go. You have to learn to do what most people are not willing to do to get to where you wish to be. Today, it is actually the easiest time in history to achieve an abundant and prosperous life because the majority are not willing to do even some of the simplest tasks with excellence. I recently spoke to a twenty-one-year-old, regional manager for one of the largest fast-food corporations in the world that was already earning a six-figure salary. How did he accomplish this super rapid rise? Consistency, effort, integrity, desire and heart.

"One of the marvels of the world is the sight of a soul sitting in a prison with the key in his hand"

Rumi

Believe in yourself. There is not a book you cannot read. There is not anything in this world you cannot attempt. There is not a skill you cannot learn. There is not a class you cannot take, especially in this digital age some are actually FREE. However, it is you that must take the first step away from who you are to move towards the who you wish to be. Choose actions every day that are in your own best interest. You are only limited by the imaginary chains you have allowed to bind you. Stop accepting less from this abundant planet than you truly deserve. You are a capable, powerful being that is deserved of receiving miracles.

"For I know the thoughts that I think toward you, says the LORD, thoughts of peace not of evil, to give you a future and a hope…, and I will bring you back from your captivity".

Jeremiah 25:11-14 NKJV

Do you know who you are? Is who you wish to be someone else? Do you aspire to be like someone else? Remember, that the icons do not mimic anyone. Remember, they are called super-stars because though there are many, they stand out and shine the brightest in the dim and dark sky. I never call them IDOLS, they are human beings, they simply decided to push beyond the constraints and made it. Just as the stars guided sailors in the evening, these super stars serve as a testament to human will and desire. You should look outward for inspiration and motivation but you must always look inward and make the decision to be YOU. Over time, if you start to make minor concessions, they will slowly take you away from your authentic self. By the time you realize you may be so far from where you wish to be.

Do you feel whole in the who you are? Do you feel firm in your stance where you are? Are you comfortable in your shoes? Every year people make a New Year resolution to change something about themselves. I have always felt that it would be incredibly powerful to resolve to be yourself. To have the courage and tenacity to be yourself in a world that is constantly telling you to be anything other than you!

Don't be like MIKE!
Do what MIKE did to become MIKE!

Resolve to become something so unique that you are excited to be you every day when you wake up. Be the protagonist in your story. The world does not need another clone. The world does not need another extra. The world does not need another NPC. What the world needs is exactly who you are. The world needs your gifts. The world needs your talents. The world needs your efforts from the heart. The world and everyone around you need you to be the real you. The world needs your passion. The world needs your love.

> **"When 99% of people doubt your idea, you're either gravely wrong or about to make history."**
>
> **Scott Belsky**

Along the way to your goals, as you get closer, I guarantee you will find that some of your closest friends and family may become adversaries or even realize they have not truly supported you. Either way, do not allow that to get you discouraged from your objective. Just because your goals in this moment might be intangible that does not mean anything. Don't falter! Just because your people do not support your vision does not mean you should not pursue it. Just because someone is in your circle, no matter how long, even if they are family does not mean that you have to stay connected. If they are a toxic presence in your life and negatively impact your mental health, they should not be a part of your future. Do not worry about people who do not exhibit the same amount of deliberate care that you do. Wisdom has shown that you should not expect anyone to ever care about you or your goals and NEVER allow that fact to CHANGE your heart or who you are destined to be. Learn to reserve your energy for those who reciprocate their connection to you through both their words and actions; those are your people.

Pay attention to who gets uncomfortable when you are working on moving up and out of old spaces. Exiting the orbit of your past will take effort to push through and out of the gravitational pull. Do not let anyone hold you down. Your closest friends and family may not see who you truly are nor do they know what you are capable of achieving. Not everyone is meant to be a part of the entire journey. Your drive to excel should not be affected in any way by the cynics, doubters, or negative people. When they are spitting their toxic negativity on your dreams you need to rise above it. Malice, pride, anger, envy, jealousy, strife, bitterness, depression, sadness and the list is endless but either you ignore or remove yourself from situations that bring out the worst in you. You will eventually be immune to anything anyone can throw at you, even family, because you are so fixed and focused on the end game. If someone attempts to obstruct your path there is no-thing that will be able to deter your forward progress.

Many of the successful report delighting in proving the naysayers wrong and use their doubt as fuel to propel them forward on their journey. Do not succumb to the devil of uncertainty. So many people internalize these negative voices and talk themselves out of their dreams. Keep imagining. Keep building. Keep moving. Keep your vision alive. A boat can only sink if it gets water inside. Do not let the water in! Do not settle for any less than you deserve. Do not let anyone or anything sink the ship that is your destiny. Never give up, keep trying and always get up more times than you fall.

PROVE THEM WRONG!

> **"What we know is a drop, what we don't know is an ocean."**
>
> **Isaac Newton**

Another secret to success is keep your visions and plans SECRET. Do not tell others your imaginations and dreams as it is likely they will not be able to see your vision. Do not to share your plans with just anyone. Until you are one-hundred percent sure they are your people; stay silent. Opt instead to work in solitude and let your success speak for itself. You may wish to disappear for a while from your present circles while you reboot, reprogram and install the new operating system of your life. Trade your nights out for enhancing your knowledge base. Trade the social club for personal intimate meaningful meetings. Trade the pursuit of things for the pursuit of your purpose and calling. Trade social media and cinema for more time to manifest your real-life happy ending. When you re-emerge…it is then time to embrace the shift.

"Be ready at any moment to give up what you are for what you might become"

W.E.B Du Bois

Know ahead of time that it is a lonely path to the top. In order for you to become a new person, you have to leave the old you behind. In order to accomplish some-thing you have never done, you have to become some-one you have never been. You have to be able to shed both the you that you are and the you that you are in the lives of others. The transformation will require you to leave the comfort and safety of your old surroundings as you expand into the unknown. Begin to build the brightest social network you can and you will then be reciprocally reflective of that luminosity. You have to fully detach. You have to fully detach from who you used to be. You have to fully detach from the past stories. You have to fully detach from the people. You have to fully detach from the places. You have to be completely open and free as you move toward your highest calling. You have permission to begin anew with the sunrise of every day, to start again, to be born again. Give yourself a pass for the past. Remember the only rope that binds you is the rope you allow. **You are liberated. You are special. You are limitless.**

THE WHEN

"The secret of getting ahead is getting started. The secret of getting started is breaking your complex overwhelming tasks into small manageable tasks, and starting on the first one."

Mark Twain

When? NOW!
Say it: RIGHT NOW!

More than two thousand years ago, Lao Tzu posited: the journey of a thousand miles begins with a single step. You must make the first move. No endeavor happens on its own. The idea will not execute itself. The exams require preparation. The yoga asanas require practice. The book will not write itself. The bricks need to be fashioned into the building. This book you are reading had its origin in ideas years before it was started and it has been almost seven years to bring it to fruition. In the interim, I published two books of poetry. The projected date of this project perpetually shifted with life BUT never the goal of its <u>completion</u>!

In preparation for this book, I read voraciously, I listened to thousands of hours of podcasts and viewed dozens of lectures. When you start you must humble yourself and realize that there is always something to learn. Everyone is your teacher and inspiration is everywhere, so pay very close attention. You also have to recognize during the process that you must choose to insert that final period, submit the manuscript to the publisher and move on to the next project. It is very easy to become too fixated that you lose focus on the end game.

> **"Humility forms the basis of honor, just as the low ground forms the foundation of a high elevation."**

> **Bruce Lee**

Do not think about where you have been or where you are right now. You have considered those notions and it the time to build your dreams upon the solid foundation of NOW. Start spending the majority of your time thinking about where you WANT to go. Stop considering your age, your educational level, your skillset, your ideologies, etc. if you are HERE that means you still have time. The NOW is your opportunity. The past is gone, the future is unknown and it is called: THE PRESENT because it is a GIFT. Life is a miracle and no future is promised to anyone. A miracle is an extraordinary event that typically occurs during times of adversity. It is in the times of hardship that you need to continue forward. It is in the times of difficulty that you need to get out of the house and experience the world. Fully embrace today and know that yesterday is not your forever. No storm lasts indefinitely. Even for Noah, it was forty days and nights of storm but on that forty-first day the rainbow appeared. It is up to you to show up, to be there, day-after-day-after-day-after-day and to be fully present. Show up for YOU.

Pull the ribbon, unwrap each day with wonder and enjoy the surprise that life brings. Yesterday does not define today. It is up to you to start fresh and begin again. Actually, take this one step further philosophically, instead of beginning again: **begin anew**.

For as long as I can remember, I never wait for special days to do special things. I have always thought of every day as being my birthday. Why wait for a special day? I do my best to live each moment with full and complete presence. Pivot your perspective and realize, it is during times of despair and desperation that your efforts and inspired action lay the groundwork for your miracles to evolve. Step into the now and engage these precious present moments consciously and deliberately.

> **"Of all the liars in the world, sometimes the worst are our own fears."**
>
> **Rudyard Kipling**

When you want to stop, is when you need to push through. When you feel when you cannot do it, is typically when you are closest. When you don't feel like working out, is when you need to go to the gym. When you want to hit the snooze bar, is when you need to jump out of bed. It is in the darkest times when you need the most willpower to push forward. NEVER EVER EVER EVER give in to your insecurities and fears; usurp your motivation and go forth full force towards your future.

Shift your perspective and begin to see problems or obstacles as opportunities and stepping-stones. You have to allow your perspective to evolve as you move towards your goals. The majority of obstacles are not physical, they are psychological. The successful are frightened. The successful have doubt. The successful weep. The successful are just like you. You have to become a mental gymnast. You have to learn to step into the I am now terrified but it is about embracing the feeling, it is about feeling the fear and it is about moving ahead despite the fear; it is about conquering it. You have to have the courage to embrace your evolutionary shift in perspective and consciousness that will be the precursor to new possibilities and miracles to manifest in your reality. You need to be receptive to change. You need to be open to new ideas. You need to realize that your thoughts, perspective and intentions are powerful tools to get you to the life of your dreams.

You do not have to be **perfect** to write a song. You do not have to be a **scholar** to write a book. You do not have to have a **degree** to start a business. You do not have to have the highest **IQ** to get a degree. You do not need any previous **training** to get your white belt. <u>What you</u>

have to do is to overcome your fear to BEGIN. TRUST ME, there will **NEVER** be a perfect moment nor is there ever a perfect time or perfect situation to begin. You have to **choose** and you have to **START**. All masters were once beginners.

Furthermore, you cannot achieve greatness if you cannot learn to operate through life's turbulence. Life like a flight is not always smooth. You, the pilot needs to focus on your goal not the obstacles. Why? Airplane pilots know that their attention is a scarce resource and in order to fly a plane it requires immense focus and multitasking skills. To focus on anything that detracts from their immediate situational awareness can lend to disaster, crash and death. The key is to take the first step. To take the next steps forward with directed and focused awareness. To fly with unwavering attention to your goal is the most direct flight to your dreams. The sky is the limit!

> **Therefore, my beloved brethren, be steadfast, immovable, always abounding in the work of the Lord, knowing that your labor is not in vain in the Lord.**
>
> **Corinthians 15:58 NKJV**

THE SEED

"Do not be deceived, God is not mocked; for whatever a man sows, that he will also reap. For he who sows to his flesh will of the flesh reap corruption, but he who sows to the Spirit will of the Spirit reap everlasting life. And let us not grow weary while doing good, for in due season we shall reap if we do not lose heart. Therefore, as we have opportunity, let us do good to all, especially to those who are of the household of faith."

Galatians 6:7-10 NKJV

I wish for you to believe that all of your dreams are available to you. You can have all that you wish. You can accomplish anything. You deserve to live your best life. The secret is that you have to imagine it first in your mind. As I stated earlier, everything that exists in the world first had a cognitive origin. I wish for you to <u>BELIEVE</u> that your dreams, goals and future all exist and they are simply waiting for you to align with them energetically so that they may manifest.

George Bernard Shaw stated: "Imagination is the beginning of creation. You imagine what you desire, you will what you imagine and at last you create what you will." You cannot have any-thing you cannot imagine. No-thing is impossible to your imagination. Your imagination is not only limitless but any-thing is possible if you have the ability to see it in your mind. Neville Goddard emphasized daily visualization practices every evening upon sleeping. He urged you must see, hear, taste, smell and feel your desires as being REAL. Your goals are like a seed but the detailed thoughts of those desires must be planted to possess the fruit.

When is the best time to plant a tree?

Twenty years ago. Ten years ago. Five years ago. NOW!

It is never too late to start the path to your best life but you must know the rocky travail that is before you. I will use the apple tree for my metaphor. Just like every apple, every success begins with the planting of a seed. It is intriguing to consider that a seed looks nothing like the apple. Your beginning will look nothing like your end. Hold an apple in your hand, it is the final phase of the seed's journey and it may be the fruit of a thirty-year-old tree.

The apple is the delicious end of an incredible metamorphosis. It is a laborious, complicated, protracted and painful process. You must be a diligent gardener of your goals. Many on the path to success tend to get impatient. Many on the path to success tend to get ahead of themselves. Many on the path to success think they can just plant a seed and then magically (poof) harvest delicious apples.

You may think the first step is to plant the seed. Just like the farmer, you must understand that it is equally imperative to know that every seed requires its own appropriate timing, season, medium and climate in order to germinate, prosper and bear fruit. Analogously, it is critical for you to bring immense clarity to who you are, where you are and what you truly desire. Bhāvana in Sanskrit means to cultivate, to develop, to manifest or to call into existence. The Buddhist traditions have a similar perspective, they emphasize the need to cultivate our mind, body and spirit like the ground so the wonderful beautiful fruits of life may emerge.

Therefore, your first step is to take the time to clean up your environment. Just as the farmer tills and fertilizes the field prior to planting, you too need to foster a rich environment that will be able to support and sustain your personal growth as you move towards your goals. You cannot plant seeds in the soil of hatred, hostility, anger, resentment, sadness, dissent, etc. and expect them to germinate and to grow in such an environment. It is time to transmute all of the garbage you have been through thus far and turn it into rich compost for your future. Trust me, all of that "stuff" you have accumulated will NOT BE WASTED. Right now, consider it as the manure to strengthen the garden of your goals. Later you will be fully aware of the reasons why. Your special seeds require their soil to be fertilized with love, joy, peace and tranquility to grow. Once you are completely honest with yourself. Once you are at peace with your past. Once you purify your motives. Once you clarify your goals. It is only then will you be ready to sow the most fruitful and beautiful orchard.

"Don't judge each day by the harvest you reap but by the seeds that you plant."

Robert Louis Stevenson

On the journey to success, one must be able to endure the same challenges that are presented the seed. Hope and faith are the fertilizer for your dreams. Once you plant the seed you must not uproot it with dissonant thoughts and doubt. Be on the offense. Build a fence. Defend your plot. Be active. Be diligent. Even the space between your ears can be a formidable pest. Be protective of anything that might threaten your destiny, it may even be your own thoughts. You do not plant the seed in your fertile ground and fixate on that plot shouting: I am waiting. You do not plant the seed and give your harvest a time limit. You do not plant a seed and dig it up to check and see how it is doing. Patience is critical to the process. You must have the ability to think in years and decades; not days. It takes time to manifest super ripe delicious fruit. You have to understand there is a gestation process. You must trust it is there and tend to it, but it will do what it naturally will do, when it naturally does it; nothing you can do will FORCE it to sprout. The seed has its own timeline. Your patience and faith will be tested. You must have the endurance of a distance runner to successfully complete the marathon that is the path to your goals. Each seed has its own timing and you must allow the universe to facilitate the orchestration of the necessary players to manifest the most beautiful symphony. Patience is critical but not passivity, there is a fine balance between patience and activity. Trust in the process and you will innately know as your intuition grows along with your seedling.

> **"And not only so, but we glory in tribulations also: knowing that tribulation worketh patience; And patience, experience; and experience, hope: And hope maketh not ashamed; because the love of God is shed abroad in our hearts by the Holy Ghost which is given unto us."**
>
> **Romans 5:3-5 KJV**

Just as you cannot rush a seed to germinate, nor can you rush your way to your dream. You cannot build a company in months; it takes on average four years to build a brand. You must accumulate ten-thousand hours to become an expert in any subject matter. We live in a fast-food culture. We live in a social media over-night-viral millionaire culture. You can focus your energy on the fast track. You can focus on the quick dollar. You can focus on the easy way. More often than not, those are the short-lived success stories. I am an end game focused, blue-chip stock invested, big juicy delicious recession proof apple farmer.

> **"The roots of education are bitter, but the fruit is sweet."**
>
> **Aristotle**

You, like the seed must go through a period of darkness and metamorphosis. You, like the seed will effort to break through the shell to sprout in the dark shadowy soil. It is a painful cracking and it is an efforted change to push through the shell. Consider how different that seed looks from the sprout that develops. Consider how different that sprout looks from the seedling. Consider how different that seedling looks from the tree. Consider how different that seed looks from the fruit. Consider that your journey will not only look different but it will also FEEL different at all stages in the process. Maintain your endurance to push through the intensely difficult dark times and be aware that it is at **this** very point where most fail.

Be aware that contrary to your logic, while the sprout is breaking through the shell into the soil, there is not only a metamorphosis but the next phase of the journey for that seedling is down. The seedling must now go deeper and force its way into the dark unknown. The seedling must plunge itself into the soil to establish firmly the root system. The take-home lesson is to acknowledge that growth is not always visible. You will have to continue your progress in faith while nurturing your growing seedling. Joel Osteen said in a sermon: **The bitter root will produce bitter fruit.** Be mindful at every stage in the process. Be mindful every day as you tend to your daily life. Be mindful that every moment is an opportunity for growth. In your world, you need to constantly enhance your skillset, expand your mindset, learn new ideologies, build your social network, listen to the podcasts, read the books, earn your degree and add distinguished lines to your resume before you can be in alignment with the life you truly desire.

> **"But he who received the seed on stony places, this is he who hears the word and immediately receives it with joy; yet he has no root in himself, but endures only for a while. For when tribulation or persecution arises because of the word, immediately he stumbles."**
>
> **Matthew 13:20-22 NKJV**

Chinese bamboo will spend approximately five years establishing a root system before sprouting. Once it does break the surface, its rise and growth are intensely rapid and relentless. It will reach its maximum height within sixty days and during this time period it has been known to stretch upwards of forty-eight inches within the span of twenty-four hours; some species you can physically witness their growth. The lesson you can take from the bamboo sprout is to be sure to establish an incredibly strong foundational root system so that when you ultimately show yourself to the world you can begin a rapid journey upward.

As a gardener, you will have to defend your seedling against invasive species. As noted above, your progress at times will be invisible but it will also be riddled with obstacles and you must have the fortitude to persist and continue despite the attacks on your garden of dreams. Every hardship and every adversity are additional opportunities to grow, if you handle each properly. **If** you stay the course and <u>push</u> you will eventually break through the shell. Push, push, push and you will eventually break through the surface to the light. The door to opportunity, like the sprout breaking through the surface will occur suddenly and when it does you **WILL KNOW IT**. It will be an undeniable moment and you will feel an incredible release and a profound increase of your personal power. Remember, if you lose faith and give up too soon, you will miss your opportunity and your sprout, your prospects and all of your efforts will wither away.

Everyone recognizes the flowers, everyone wishes to enjoy the fruit, everyone wishes to possess the material manifestations but what most do not recognize is that success is a long-term cumulative process. Determination is necessary. Faith is necessary. FOCUS is necessary. Focus on your soil before planting the seed. Focus on your roots before your flowers. Focus on your flowers before your fruit. Follow **O**ne **C**ourse **U**ntil **S**uccessful. It will take consistent gardening, which involves constant watering, fertilizing, nurturing and pruning. Note that the work does not cease once your tree begins to bear fruit. Your next level work begins at the harvest and continues then season after season; your ceiling becomes your next floor. A saying that is attributed to Al Capone is applicable here: Do not shake the green apple tree, when the apple is ripe it will fall down by itself. **Do not force the process.**

> Everything originates from the sowing of seeds with DETERMINATION. Striving for success without putting in the hard work is like trying to harvest where you have not planted. Expecting the seed to grow without watering is certain failure. Expecting the branches to produce the most fruit without pruning is to deny your maximum harvest. It is important to prune your social network to align yourself with your

forthcoming season. Old dry branches will not be able to support the weight of the new opportunities. Cutting away the dead will make room for new connections and support systems. As well, pruning will simultaneously strengthen and deepen your existing associations. Do you want your almost dreams?

or

Do you want your most grand unimaginable future?

You, like the field of dreams will experience the storms. You, will have the hurricanes of LIFE sweep through your town. It is up to you to be so firmly rooted, strong, focused, determined and resilient during the adverse times that you are minimally affected.

> No seed, no plant
> No rain, no flowers
> No flowers, no fruit

I wish for you to be so firmly planted that you are like that house that is still standing when every other home on the block was leveled. I wish for you to be the miracle, even **if** your house is devastated that you emerge unscathed without a scratch. The key is to be steady in the unsteady, to be stable in the instability and to be constant in the crisis. I wish for you to be duly prepared for the task. We always plan for success but prepare for failure. I promise that hardship and doubt will arrive but know they are temporary. I promise that life will bring you to your knees, but you will recognize that is part of the test and you will persevere with faith, focus, patience, persistence and determination.

"When patterns are broken, new worlds emerge."

Tuli Kupferberg

Most people when it comes time to decide, instead of making the tough choice, most people choose to remain in their comfort zone and they ultimately become farmers in the fields of others. Remember, deciding <u>not</u> to act is also a decision. You will be scared. You are allowed to be scared and you have to choose to RISE to the occasion; step up and WORK EVERY DAY. Sift, sort, select, sow, nurture and only then can you reap the harvest that is your dream life. Learn, change, grow, evolve, produce and serve.

> **"Then God blessed them, and God said to them, "Be fruitful and multiply; fill the earth and subdue it; have dominion over the fish of the sea, over the birds of the air, and over every living thing that moves on the earth."**
>
> **Genesis 1:28 NKJV**

THE HOW: PART I

The final section of the book you will learn to practice what I have been preaching. Do know that all of these strategies and exercises have been applied by the author. However, the old adage: "different strokes for different folks" applies; strategies that work for some may not work for others. One thing to state here is that my personal path to success was incredibly disjointed. I was learning as I was going, though I would not change a single aspect of my glorious, victorious journey and process. You may be able get to your goals faster or even overshoot your own expectations as the tools and the wisdom in this book are amassed from my almost fifty years on the planet. Lastly, this book is a testament to my legacy here on this planet. Faith without works is dead.

Let's get started! Success begins first in the mind. Success begins in our imagination. Meditation is a crucial part of the process. Meditation will be your tool in many aspects of life. It will help you to find your goals. It will help you find your direction. I will help you maintain your focus. It will help you unlock your gifts. It will help you find peace in the most trying of times. It will help you find yourself when you are lost. You are all that which you desire and that all things that you can fully envision are possible. Every single person on the planet has innate gifts and a divine purpose <u>but</u> so many do not do the work to unearth those jewels. Seek and ye shall find. So many people live such distracted lives that they do not take the time to reach within themselves. So many people are fixated on the external that they ignore what is right there in front of them.

Earl Nightingale tells the story of an African farmer who dreamed of wealth. A simple farmer, he wished to have the prosperity he heard about in the stories told of diamond mining. He decided to sell his farm and set off on a life prospecting for diamonds. It was not what he had imagined. It was a life of desperation as he fixated on those precious gems. Long story short, he was unsuccessful in his search but the person who paid a small price for his farm found on that property one of the most productive diamond mines on the continent. The moral of the story, do not ignore where you are right now. You may very well be sitting in the middle of a diamond mine. It is up to you to seek. It is up to you to find. It is up to you to unearth those desires and gifts (right where you STAND) that will bring you the greatest fulfillment and unimaginable wealth.

"Time stays long enough for anyone who will use it."

Leonardo da Vinci

You need a solid vision for yourself. What do you see three years, five years, ten years from right now?

Think about not taking action. Think about who will you be, think about where will you be without effort. Do you like what you see? Time is precious. Invest your time to find the inspiration and then take immediate action towards that future. Hasty and unfocused action is **not** what I am suggesting. A Spanish saying sums up my general approach to life: *Festina Tarde*: make haste slowly. Get going promptly but begin your pursuit with intent. Move both fast and wisely. Action is imperative, but it is focused inspired grounded action that is the most productive. Do not be fooled into rushing as greatness like the best wine takes time. Time is of the essence. Time is not an unlimited resource. Time is the most precious commodity. Time well spent is crucial. Time spent wisely will pay dividends. How many years do you have left? How many chances do you have left? The task of this book is to help you get to the place where you can FOCUS: **F**oster **O**riginality, **C**reativity and **U**nderstanding of **S**elf. The average person has thirty-thousand days on the planet and it is time to take the time and put your brief life in perspective.

> **"By letting go, it all gets done; The world is won by those who let it go!"**
>
> **Lao Tzu**

GET YOUR JOURNAL! Identify your goals. Identify the skills you need to achieve those goals. Identify the timeline to learn the skills that will begin to close the gap between who you are now and who you wish to be. Let go fully of your present identity to be able to be who you are destined to be. You cannot do something you have yet to accomplish without changing your blueprint. Change your mind and change your life.

> **Procrastination is the thief of time. Collar him!"**
>
> **Charles Dickens**

Procrastination is death to your future. The only thing you should procrastinate is procrastination. What is it that you are procrastinating? Why are you putting it off? Return to your journal again and address what are your goals? Deepen your why? Once you have truly solidified your why you will be able to endure any how that comes across your path.

Your daily agenda holds the "secret" to success. In your journal document your day. What is your daily routine? What are your daily rituals? Write down things you do every day. What things do you do several times a week? What things do you do monthly? What time do you wake? What time do you go to sleep? What do you do in between? What time do you eat your snacks and meals? The essence of documenting the details is to start to get serious about maximizing every day.

Be a good chef and begin to evaluate your intellectual kitchen: clear it, clean it, disinfect it, and polish it. You need to always keep moving forward. Your life and daily routine is analogous to preparing a meal. To cook a complete meal in the kitchen, you have to balance several things on the stovetop and in the oven. All of the dishes are simultaneously cooking at various speeds, so timing, balance and focus are essential for success.

FOCUS: Find Organize Clarify Understand Select

Timing is everything in life. You need to learn to multitask. You need to learn to tend to all of the items on the stove: checking, adjusting, stirring and most importantly completing those tasks before they spoil.

- Understand laziness is a perspective
- Every person in the world will suffer the same fate
- Close your browser
- Spend one hour every day learning
- Choose to practice
- Choose to improve
- Choose to not take the easy way out

Do not mistake difficulties or challenges as things to avoid. Difficulties are your opportunities to face, rise and overcome. There is power in practice. Continuous practice and repetition are the key to mastery. As a yoga teacher I say to my students, it is yoga practice not yoga perfect. However, with continuous practice and dedication you will eventually perfect the asana. As well, there is a saying practice does not make perfect: perfect practice makes perfect. Bikram Choudhury has a saying: Do little and do right! Always focus on the proper way and build from there your strong foundation. Every time you approach your life you need to bring full attention to the tasks at hand.

Inherit the future or suffer the past.

Tragedy is a part of life. The essential truth is that you can rise above your history to your brightest future. Just because something takes longer than you expected, or longer than others to complete, is not indicative of failure. Just because life happens, keep on life-ing. You are on YOUR schedule, not anyone else's. Life is not a competition against others, it is a competition against yourself and your clock is ticking; it is YOU versus YOU. Your competition is you versus your bad habits. Your competition is you versus your distractions. Your competition is you versus your procrastination. Your competition is you versus your disbelief. Your competition is you versus your insecurities. Your competition is you versus your fears. Your competition is you versus your ego. Your competition is against your neglect of self. To get to your juiciest reality, rise above your limitations and go from **"negative to positive"** like Christopher George Latore Wallace. You are infinitely creative but stop restricting your clarity and potential by focusing on the heckling of your inner voices. Cultivate knowledge, increase your awareness and raise the bar of your own expectations. Have a funeral for your past life and prior expectations. Nothing in your past looks like your future. Be Moses and say to yourself: **Let my people go! (Exodus 5:1)**

"No man is free who cannot control himself."

Pythagoras

Be honest with yourself. You are where you are because of the choices you've made up to this point in your life. What is your current narrative? You can change the story if you really desire to. You still have time to author a brilliant chapter in your life story! Do you believe that you can overcome the walls of Jericho? Are you aware of your abilities? Are you aware of your freedom? Are you aware of your sovereignty? Remember the story of the elephant and do not be tethered by the past. Uproot the rope and create a new future you are stronger than you know. Deep desire, vision and sacrifice are the trifecta for winning the race to your goals.

Be a warrior, <u>not</u> a worrier.

Make the rest of your days, the <u>best</u> of your days.

You didn't come this far to only come this far, <u>do not settle</u>, push for more.

You can either quit or keep going; they both hurt.

You are a survivor, <u>not</u> a quitter.

Read these phrases again and again until you believe them.

You may have quit. You may have lacked commitment. You may have squandered opportunity. You may have wasted time. Look back for just a brief moment and embrace the present. You were not ready then. Consider the past as a set up for the right now. Consider the past as preparation for this moment. Consider the past failures and experiences as motivation to <u>not</u> give up <u>this goal</u>.

Seek growth, seek greatness and seek the challenge. If the journey wasn't challenging, the destination wouldn't be as great. The most difficult paths, lead to the most beautiful destinations. Our minds have the ability to create any mental state of our choosing. Today you need to forget the reasons and excuses you used in the past when you decided to quit. Today you need to find the tenacity, courage and faith to succeed no matter what comes your way. **PRONOIA.** Believe that everything around you is conspiring to assist you on the path to your dreams. Believe that success is your birthright. It will not be easy, but I guarantee that <u>it will be worth it</u>. It will be worth all of the time, blood, sweat, tears and prayers. Success is never a straight line. Success is never along an unencumbered path. You are a warrior and must fight through the gauntlet to your destiny.

COMMITMENT. I have lived my life since the age of sixteen according to an axiom that was posted on my High School wrestling room wall: **The harder you work, the luckier you get.** I discovered while researching for this book that the quote is attributed both to Mike Adenuga and Joe Ricketts. Mike is a Nigerian billionaire businessman who ranks presently as the sixth wealthiest person on the continent of Africa. Joe used the phrase as the title for his memoir and details the path to his thirty-billion-dollar company that had its origins on borrowed money from his faithful friends and family. Lucius Annaeus Seneca the Younger, an ancient Roman philosopher similarly postulated: **Luck is what happens when preparation meets opportunity.** Robert Balden-Powell in 1907 initiated the Scout motto: Be Prepared. In an interview he was asked: Be prepared for what? He urged the need to be prepared for "any old thing." He wrote in 1908 in Scouting for Boys: You are always in a state of readiness in mind and body to do your duty. Are you prepared? Are you ready? In the years compiling ideas for this book, I discovered a complementary quote on the path: **The harder you work, the harder it is to surrender.**

Do you want to be extra-ordinary? If so, you cannot let the days pass without giving it your all. The pessimist wondered why the glass was half empty. He did not consider the time that was spent thinking about the question he was allowing the water he did have to evaporate. Most people will give a little effort. Many people give as little effort as possible. Most people will give a little time. Many people will give as little time as possible. All of these people still wonder why they are not winning. All of these people wonder why they are unhappy with their lives. Winners work as hard as possible every day and always question if they can do **MORE**. Winners are constantly seeking to up-level. Winners are always doing their absolute best wherever they are at the moment. Do you do more than what you are paid for? Do you work beyond your job description? How much value do you bring to your place of employment? Do you push past your limits? Do you work as hard as you possibly can in everything you endeavor? Do you feel a sense of pride in what you do? Take the time to journal and address your life and achievements up to this point in your life. Do you do the little things in life with careful attention? Do you work as hard when your boss isn't watching?

Are you a lion or a gazelle? Be the lion when the others are contented to be gazelles. We live in a culture today that even with half efforts you can be quite successful. So many people are contentedly happy being mediocre gazelles because they did not get consumed by the lion *today!*

You can survive, you can make it, you can have a decent life just by staying with the herd. All you have to do is to not be the slowest gazelle. If you want to be extra-ordinary, you have to separate yourself from the masses. If you want to be extra-ordinary, you have to give *everything* you have in *everything* you do, every day. Do you. Be you. Be real. Be true. Be strong. Be courageous.

<u>BE A LION</u>

If you do not push, you will miss the opportunities and you may miss the chance of a lifetime. Never take a single day of your life for granted, as opportunities typically **do not** present themselves twice.

What are your personal standards? Do you have the highest expectations and standards? You need to impose a standard of excellence in everything you do. Every task, no matter how small should be completed with the utmost care because you never know who is watching. Integrity is a critical personal quality and at its essence is doing the right thing when no one is watching. Be the best at what you do. Do your best and stop seeking validation for what you do. You do not get in life what you want, you get in life what you are. You are a perfect reflection of the sum total of your choices. Do you wish to reflect hard work and effort or the opposite?

Impact drives income. You are paid for your value, not by the hour. Strive every day to increase your value in the marketplace. Push yourself to a point that <u>you</u> have never been before. You cannot go to new places if you don't move. The ship <u>must</u> leave the harbor! Prepare for uncharted territory.

Decide, Commit, Resolve.

The true measures of wealth and success:

- Who are you beyond what you see in the mirror?
- How do you describe yourself beside what you do?
- What are you worth without your money?
- How will you be remembered?
- Will you leave a legacy?

You are the author and you decide the story. You decide the script and storyline. Do not be an extra in another's movie. Do not get muddled in an obscure role in the plot and expectations of others. Step up and take the pen, take control and begin to write your own narrative. Beat pro-crastination! Be pro-active! Be the pro-tagonist in your story!

<u>Commitment</u>

Here is that word again! Are you fully committed? Do you just go through the motions? Are you truly invested in your goals? Have you ever gone **all in**? We live in a very casual culture. As a sociologist, I have witnessed a shift towards a very laisse-faire approach to life. It is not necessarily a "bad" thing to have some sense of "non-attachment", and it is good to stay open to options and opportunity. But, I feel we are using this concept as an excuse and an easy out to detract from responsibility and accountability; and therein lies the problem. We see it across the board in relationships, education, hobbies and goals; the reluctance to commit <u>completely</u>. The majority of my success has been possible through the <u>full commitment</u> to any task at hand, no matter what they be. If I was in a relationship, they were "the one", until they were not. The same could be said for my education, work, career and even my pastimes...**LIVE FULL and DIE EMPTY**. The <u>could be</u> of your dreams <u>might be</u> trapped behind your level of commitment.

> **"Courage is not having the strength to go on; it is going on when you don't have the strength."**
>
> **Teddy Roosevelt**

Seriously be honest with yourself about your work ethic. Forget the journal and head over to the nearest mirror. How do you show up? How hard do you work? What adjectives do people use when they talk about you? Have you ever been acknowledged for your work ethic? Are you willing to work at something until your weakness becomes a strength? Do you run the day or does the day run you? Talent does not always succeed, it is the person who continuously efforts that will prosper. You have to get in the dirt, sometimes literally and work through the challenges to make it; despite hardships and delayed gratification the success battle is won not always with skill but with sheer **GRIT**.

Greatness Revealed In Truth

Greatness does not begin with glamour. Greatness is not achieved with popularity. Greatness is an accumulation of small tasks continuously completed with excellence. Greatness is built. Greatness does not seek; it attracts. You must face your adversity until it no longer exists.

Failure Rejection Criticism Disappointment Discouragement

No gain without pain. Embrace the pain because it is NOT your enemy. I learned from a Marine the phrase: Pain is weakness leaving the body. Even in yoga, the asanas are not a comfortable place to be and at times you will experience pain sensations. You may call it what you wish, my colleague Tim uses the term: therapeutic discomfort but at the end of the day it is simply pain. You need to push through the pain to increase your flexibility. You need to push through the pain to get to the savasana. If you do not learn to have control over the pain, then the pain will have control over you. Do your best to stay the course and know the pain will not last forever. The best medicine is to be sure to take care of your spiritual, emotional and physical being so you may endure the trials along the way.

> **"The secret of change is to focus all of your energy not on fighting the old, but on building the new."**
>
> **Socrates**

No matter what you do there will ALWAYS be people who will criticize you. Regardless of your social position or achievements critics abound. JK Rowling, the author of the Harry Potter series and self-identified: Billionaire in denial was rejected by twelve publishers before being accepted. Do not let anyone tell you that you are: not good enough, too old, too young, too short, too skinny, too weak…etc. Never fear the verdict. You decide what you will accept in your life. You cannot fear rejection. You cannot let criticism define you. A resilient person will persevere in the face of fear. You have to let your disappointments when they do arise to teach you. You have to let your disappointments when they do arise to <u>fuel you</u>. Let the history of those who came before you guide you. Know that if you consistently continue forward with pure passion and determination, you will find a place in this world.

Allow your pain to permeate and push you beyond where you are to where you wish to be. Your pain is part of the journey and you must harness your will to get through the difficult days. Excuses are dangerous! No one cares about your excuses but I can guarantee the pain will be greater if you do not decide to accomplish your dreams. It is in those difficult moments that your character is developed. You decide in those moments that your goals are as important as life itself.

<u>The enemy is your inner me</u>

There is an African proverb that states: **When there is no enemy within, the enemy outside cannot harm you.** You have the power to deal with what is going on around you. The mind is the battle ground. The battle is between your ears and behind your eyes. You have to be as vigilant shielding your spiritual and emotional well-being as you do with your physical body. Similarly consider this adage: **Ships do not sink because of the water around them, they sink when the water gets in them.** Doubt and hesitation will disrupt your drive, derail your path and destroy your dreams. Doubt has its roots in fear. Our personal history has conditioned us to fear loss and suffering but what are you willing to risk to achieve your goals. Nothing risked means nothing gained. Are you ready for the next level? **<u>Are you really ready for the next level?</u>** Stay dedicated, impose your will because the water is not always going to be smooth. If you are serious about what you are trying to do. You have to "choose" to endure whatever crosses your path. You cannot expect things to always be calm, it is exactly the opposite.

Remember:
Diamonds are formed under immense pressure.
Grapes must be crushed to make wine.
Olives are pressed to extract oil.

Whenever you feel the weight of life upon you, you need to KNOW that you are in the right place. Personally, I have found that the closer you get to your goals the more difficult things become. The book you are reading forced me at every turn to practice everything written in these pages! You have what it takes <u>but</u> do you have the strength to get there. Expect there to be turbulence and it is up to YOU to decide every day that you will push through. You learn from the lows how to ride the highs. You must learn to maintain your composure under pressure so the correct steps and directions are clear. One of life's greatest challenges is having control over your emotions. The person who perseveres rises above the challenges; you need to push through. You will be remembered for what you accomplish, not the process. No one cares what you are going through. No one cares about the touchdown you almost scored. No one cares about the degree you almost earned. No one cares about the book you almost published. You do not lose anything as long as you learn through the process and level up. Dedicate yourself, have a willingness to commit, show up and get through the challenges; grow through the changes and press on. One word summary: **PERSISTENCE.**

THE HOW: PART II

Grab your journal. It is time to get real with yourself. How much time have you wasted? How much time do you have to make up for? I do not see time as truly wasted as long as you can reflect and learn from your experiences. How much have you grown since last year? If you are reading this book then this is your wake-up call. It is time to now maximize the time you have been gifted. It is time to reflect on the time you have left. It is time to prioritize your life. It is time to evaluate your priorities. It is time for you to be the you that you wish to be. The secret to the how is the now.

> **"A man's gift makes room for him, And brings him before great men."**
>
> **Proverbs 18:16 NKJV**

What is your state of being? Are you living for you? Streaming programming, social media, video games...these distractions not only cost you monetarily but they cost you your precious time. These distractions cost you your precious time that you could be dedicating to your future and dreams. What are you doing right now to achieve your goals? What did you accomplish thus far today? How much of life do you feel is in your control? Do you feel life is controlling you? Do you feel anxious? Do you feel restless? Is what you <u>say</u> aligned with what you are <u>actually doing</u>? Is what you are <u>doing</u> aligned with what you <u>desire</u>?

You can say you wish to be healthier, but are you working out several times a week? You can say you want a better job but are you working as hard as you possibly can to get a promotion. You need to evaluate your schedule and see if you are actually telling yourself the truth about why you are not in the physical shape you wish to be in. You need to evaluate your daily schedule and be sure that it is aligned with your desires and goals. Talk is cheap. Consistent action is ESSENTIAL. Take control of your calendar and schedule time for the things that matter most in your life: present and future.

> **"Beware of little expenses. A small leak will sink a great ship."**
>
> **Benjamin Franklin**

There is no right time, the time <u>is</u> right now! It is not only the time to begin but it is time to take seriously your future. It is important to look to the time from now until retirement. It is very important to begin to SAVE SAVE SAVE for your future. How can you embrace an opportunity if you cannot pay for it? How can you garner a return if you have nothing to invest? We live in a culture that impresses upon us the urge to SPEND and makes it incredibly EASY to waste your precious resources. We live in a culture that downplays the horrific consequences of debt. We are constantly tempted to give in to the short-term desire. Yes, the immediate gratification is delicious in that moment but there is always a price: time and money.

> **"You must gain control over your money or the lack of it will forever control you."**
>
> **Dave Ramsey**

You spent how much on your expensive watch but how much did it <u>cost</u> you to watch the time sweep past? Invest in you! Invest in your future. Before you make a purchase, consider how it benefits you and if it is truly needed. The cost of watching that series was equivalent to the time you could have been working out. The cost of eating out once is equivalent to multiple days of healthy meals. The cost of a night on the town is equivalent to the cost of a personal training session. The cost of a GUCCI belt is equivalent to a coaching seminar. Streamline your life and learn to maximize your resources, which will ultimately help you maximize your most precious resource: TIME. Take the time now to return to your journal and consider your present priorities. My late friend John Ostwald shared with me one day a golden nugget of wisdom from his counseling career. There was an extremely successful business owner who was having trouble at home with his spouse and their marriage was in crisis. John presented him a question: a relationship is like a business, if you wish for that business to succeed you must put your time, energy and resources into it, you must invest in it. Do you put the same energy into your marriage as you do your company? The same analogy applies to your dreams, you must <u>invest in them</u> if you truly wish for them to flourish. Are you investing fully in your future? Everyone desires freedom. Everyone has a different definition of freedom. To me the ultimate freedom is the freedom from debt. And… FREEDOM is expensive!

Do not WASTE your resources prematurely!
You have to pay yourself back for the time
and resources you squandered.
Design your day, weeks, months and years to create value in your life.

You have to forgive yourself but never forget the past. You have to take the time to remember the past in order to make the necessary adjustments now. Take some time to document in your journal the regrets and "should-haves" of your life thus far. Do not look at them and feel bad about them, instead use those mishaps and deficiencies to fuel your future. Use your past to light an unrelenting flame to push you to be your best self. It is from this point forth and only this point forth you can live. You cannot change the past and the only value your past has for you now is to extrapolate its lessons. Pick up the pieces, put yourself back together, make peace with your past and most importantly make peace with yourself. It is now the time for you to think big. It is now the time for you to dream big.

"We don't drift into good directions. We discipline and prioritize ourselves there."

Andy Stanley

Start now! Get it done! Are you sick of the grind? then…that means keep grinding. Are you sick of going through the motions? then…. that means keep going through the motions. Always focus on forward motion and progress until things open up for you. Once you begin, the minutes turn into hours, the hours turn into days, the days turn into weeks, the weeks turn into years and the once novice becomes the expert. The secret of success is in your daily routine. Consistency is the key to success. You will face difficulty. You will face challenges. Do not go back, do not retreat. Hold the vision of your goal. You already looked back, you have to keep moving forward. The rearview mirror in your car is small for a reason, keep your hand on the wheel and your eyes forward. As you move through the challenges, you will make breakthroughs. Do not miss the sparks of creativity and insights that occur. Pay attention as these are the path altering moments that will steer you toward new knowledge and wisdom. Learn to keep your journal close by so you do not lose those epiphanies. These moments have the potential to be both transformative and serve as catalysts to your highest path and calling.

You may very well fall, but never fall back, always fall forward. Do not look back, always look forward. Look at your everyday life. Consistently review your to-do list and complete tasks. Actually, do that right now. Get back to those first pages in your journal and assess what you have compiled thus far. Remember, every day you are working on your harvest and you cannot reap what you do not sow. Focus on the end result. Focus on who you want to become. Focus on your environment. What are you trying to accomplish? What are your goals? Focus is everything. Focus equals power.

Fixed Ongoing Concentration for Unlimited Success

Focus…is a pathway to creativity. Maintain your momentum. Focus… is a decision. Force yourself to behave differently than you feel. No one has ever felt bad after completing a task. Maintain your to-do list and check off your boxes. The key is to stay in a positive state of mind. You are not going to feel "good" every day, but do it anyway. You are not always going to be motivated every day, but do it anyway. The temporary pain is always worth the long-term success. Be the most disciplined lazy person. You are not going to WANT to do it every day but just get up and make progress because you are aware of the <u>consequences of inaction</u>.

"With faith, discipline and selfless devotion to duty, there is nothing worthwhile that you cannot achieve."

Muhammad Ali Jinnah

Discipline is the bridge between thought and accomplishment. Discipline is the bridge between inspiration and value. Discipline is the bridge between strategy and productivity. Productivity is never an accident. Productivity is the disciplined and focused use of your time. Harness your willpower and get over the hump of starting, whatever it may be. It is possible to change your entire direction and destiny by choice. You never know what each day will bring, whom you might meet or what possibilities there are unless you are out there in the world. Get up and get active. All of your goals are upstream, do not drift, do not just go with the flow; start rowing and maintain your constant focus and effort to your dreams. Self-discipline is at the heart of all material success. You cannot win the war against the world if you cannot win the war against yourself. Perform to the best of your abilities. Keep your commitments. Keep your promises to yourself and others. Meet all of your deadlines. Take full responsibility for your life.

"Seek freedom and become captive of your desires. Seek discipline and find your liberty."

Frank Herber

Make adjustments and never make excuses. Neglect and excuses are cumulative and will add up exponentially over time. Some opportunities will never present themselves again in your lifetime. You want to be able to be in the position to accept them and you can only do so if and only if they are even offered to you. Here are some of the most common excuses I have heard that you need to eradicate from your script.

I'll start tomorrow
I don't have the time
I don't have a car
I don't have a passport
I don't have the money
I don't care
I don't know what to do
I have to work
It's not my fault
I'm too old
I'm too young
I'm not smart enough
It's not fair
I'm tired
I'll do it later
I was going to do it but...
I have to focus on my family
It is a work in progress
I have too much going on
Life is too complicated right now

There isn't always tomorrow. You need to change your perspective and eliminate all excuses. Have the courage to start. Have the discipline to DO THE BEST JOB YOU CAN. Have the resolve knowing that you will make mistakes. Have the compassion to know that you are human. Have the belief that you are capable of accomplishing any task you set your mind to. Have the willpower to DO IT ANYWAY, even when you don't <u>feel</u> like it! Have the strength to work through the pain. Have the consistency to work through the weakness. Have the determination to work through the urge to quit. Have the drive to work through the tired and knowing that rest is waiting for you when you have completed your tasks for the day.

"Live your life while you have it. Life is a splendid gift. There is nothing small in it. For the greatest things grow by God's law out of the smallest. But to live your life, you must discipline it."

Florence Nightingale

GETTING REST is important as YOU CANNOT FILL FROM AN EMPTY CUP and it is imperative to develop healthy lifestyle habits. Healthy lifestyle habits will not only enhance your ability to produce but simultaneously will increase your longevity to be able to enjoy the fruits of your labor. As long as you are both physically and mentally strong, you will become an unstoppable force. It is impossible to reach your greatest potential if you are not at your best both physically and mentally. Start with SELF LOVE and SELF CARE. BUT sometimes you will need to work, effort and push through tired. You will have nights where you fall asleep with a book in your hand because you gave it your all that day. Your goals are a matter of life and death. You will not progress toward your goals without work. If you work on your gifts, they will multiply and give you the greatest return on your investment. Do not go to sleep when you are tired, you go to sleep when you are DONE! Your life is YOUR responsibility. We seem to have the very skewed notion that we always have more time. Life is NOT a GAME. There is NO RESET BUTTON. Take a moment to return to your journal and consider these questions. Have you ever put your all into what you do? Are you satisfied with how you have lived your life?

Loyalty / Integrity / Dignity / Self-worth / Self-esteem / Self-respect

All of these aspects of your identity and personality are your responsibility. As well they are determined and developed by your choices that either contribute or detract from your character and reputation. How much influence do you have in the world? If you wish to increase your influence in the world then you must consider these intangible yet extremely valuable personal assets. You have to be organized in everything you do. You have to be focused in everything you do. You have to be consistent in everything you do and the key to being your best you is learning to maximize your twenty-four hours each day.

"A man who dares to waste one hour of time has not discovered the value of life."

Charles Darwin

It is not an official goal if it does not have a clock. The clock does not have to be the villain in your story. However, it very easily can be your downfall and let's not even consider that at this time, pun intended. You need to think of your watch as your trusty sidekick. You need to make time your best friend. Time is the divine metronome for us to set our daily tempo. Do not watch the clock, but use it to your benefit. Be a good steward of your time. Garner advantage over and against your antihero: PROCRASTINATION.

The antidote for the poison of procrastination is discipline. Discipline accomplishes the task right now. Discipline is the gateway to freedom. Discipline equals freedom. Financial freedom is one of the many gifts of grace for a disciplined life. One of the crucial shifts will be to establish a healthy relationship with your schedule. Jim Rohn once said: **there is no aristocracy of time.** Everyone gets the same twenty-four hours but what are you going to do with your time. A disciplined regimen of getting up early will help you to maximize your day, to utilize the gift that is time, more wisely.

"The future comes slowly, the present flies and the past stands still forever."

Friedrich Schiller

You are running out of time. Your relevant years are shrinking faster than you can comprehend. Your window to accomplish what you wish to accomplish is closing whether you want it to or not. It is now the time to take ownership and control of your time. It takes consistent effort to manage your valuable time. Convert your time into value. Invest in your day. Use your time to invest in you! Be sure your activities are worthy of your precious time. Time is your most valuable resource and should be treated as such. Do not let the day slip away because along with those hours will be your effectiveness. Do not let the day slip away because you will compound your tasks for the next day and simultaneously your frustration and anxiety.

You do not have the time to do nothing! Harness the day from the start and have your plan set and your focus certain. Get into your journal and review your goals. Get into your journal and sharpen your focus. Get into your journal and clarify your timeframes. Be sure your goals have a due date. Carve out time to plan, strategize and begin. Set your alarms and set daily, weekly, monthly reminders on your phone to keep you on track. Either you plan your day or your day will be planned by someone else; or worse, you will spend the day racing towards the sunset. Work your day job and simultaneously moonlight on your envisioned dream job. Once your vision begins to provide provision then you can initiate a transition plan onto your new path.

How old will you be in ten years?
The future will arrive with or without your participation.

Focused discipline, intense intent and obdurate accountability are the personality traits you must develop in order to make your dreams a reality. You must have an unwavering desire for the day, every day. You must have a mindset development strategy in place for the start of each day. You must have a plan to get from point A to point B. Return to your journal, <u>re-view</u> what you have written and see what you can clarify and refine.

Consider this: if you have not reached the destination you desire it may not be your goal, it may simply be your strategy. Mindset is everything. Read every day! Be a voracious reader and learn everything you can about the field you are interested in mastering. Learn about the key players past and present within your area of interest. Assume nothing! Do your due diligence. Research consistently because these new life challenges require you to possess new knowledge and new skills. Imagine crossing paths with a legend, you have read their book and you are able to engage an in-depth conversation about your particular interests in the field. Imagine that the conversation leads to a collaboration that would change the entire course of your career and life. It does not happen instantly, so you have to develop your pathway towards upward evolution. You have to be prepared. You have to be ready. You have to be in the right place, at the right time and in the right head-space to be able answer the door when opportunity knocks. Expertise in any field of endeavor takes thousands of hours, which is why your why is immensely important to solidify. You have a choice in every moment of your life: evolve or descend.

Start today, start small and reverently enjoy the little victories as they will cumulatively expand into the large accomplishments. Appreciating the small wins will enable you to stay motivated and find the necessary endurance to continue forth. Deny not the day of small things. You cannot be granted more if you are not diligent over the tasks you have presently. Great people do the small things excellently. In my entire career I never disrespected (privately or publicly) my employer / coach / teacher / mentor. I may not have agreed with their methods but I knew there was always something to learn. I knew there was a reason they were at the helm of their job / field / class and I was eager to learn from them. I always appreciate an individual's position, expertise and wisdom. Learning is a perpetual and limitless endeavor.

Excellence is something that is nurtured. It us up to you to find the lessons and wisdom in every moment if you are to get to where you desire to be. Life is like a kindergarten game of leapfrog. Find the wisdom in where you are right now. Get into your journal and assess the people in your life at this very moment and schedule conversations with your network. As you begin to take control of your life, you will learn to use the clock, your contacts and the calendar to your advantage. Every tick of the clock should initiate inspiration. Every tick of the clock should have you realize that every moment is a sacred gift.

"Practice like you've never won. Play like you've never lost."

Michael Jordan

Life should be a mission. Find your purpose. Find your focus. Find your drive. Voraciously working on your goals is the entry level cost to success. You must have a hunger to get there! The poet Lil Wayne once said: **I'm hungry like I didn't eat.** Sociologically, the immigrant will sometimes piggyback the native because they are literally driven by hunger. You either you maintain your hunger as you grow or you DIE! People that are hungry are truly unstoppable. Do not have the delusion that there will ever be a convenient time or that things will eventually be easy. Keep grinding!

YOU MUST APPLY DISCIPLINE AND CONSISTENCY EVERYDAY
Day to Day
Week to Week
Month to Month
Year to Year

I cannot say it enough: Consistency is key. Consistency is critical. Consistency is what will put you on the most direct track to greatness. There are no shortcuts to being the best **<u>you</u>** can be. Consistency is what turns the ordinary person into someone extraordinary. You can become someone even you could not imagine. If you spend a minimum of eighteen minutes a day focusing on one particular skill, within a year you will be well beyond a beginner and depending upon your personal abilities and intellect, you will now have a firm grasp and competency in that arena. The success pathway flows from knowledge, to experience and then to wisdom; from mind, to body, to soul. What is in your heart? Embrace your passion and you will find your mission. Moreover, I have found that if your heart is always pointing in the right direction and you are resolutely determined, you will <u>never</u> FAIL. You just FAIL FORWARD every time. Another not-so secret to success is to connect your heart to every action you take. Directly connect your heart to your goals and love will guide the way.

I have learned that it is indeed true that there are only two things sure in our culture: death and taxes. As we engage our lives we will be presented with the gifts of the living and we must remember that:

Life is both suffering and happiness

Life is, and will always be, both painful and blissful. We have to prepare ourselves for what life is and what life will present us regardless of our tax bracket. The gift and privilege of being alive is that these trials are part of your journey. You on the path to success must learn to embrace all of life and irrespective of circumstances to become a "no matter what" person. No matter how bad. No matter what the challenge. No matter why it happened. No matter who it was. No matter how you feel. You must continue to get up, take those steps and KEEP GOING! Make a "no matter what" attitude a part of your daily vitamin regimen. Remember that persistence is critical. You have to follow through and not give up too soon. Perhaps for the first time ever it is time to take absolute control and to make your life meaningful!

"To live is the rarest thing in the world; most people just exist"

Oscar Wilde

Are you just doing the bare minimum? Are you just going through the motions? Are you willing to do what you need to do to be successful? Robin S Sharma once said: **Don't live the same year seventy-five times and call it a life.** You have to open your eyes. You have to open your heart. You have to be open to new experiences and opportunities. If you want to reflect back on your life as a life well-lived then think seriously about the changes that you need to initiate. Once you begin, you will begin to see the path unfold. Success always leaves clues along the way if you are paying attention.

WELCOME ALL EXPERIENCES…
YOU NEVER KNOW WHAT THIS NEW DAY WILL BRING

How are you looking at your life? You are in complete control of your life. Wayne Dyer and many others have said: change the way you look at things and the things you look at will change. I urge you to shift your perspective. It is time to make those changes, to shift your perspective, to: **Think Differently.** You need to think like the person you wish to become, not the person you are. You need to completely shift your mindset and set your compass to where you want to go. Moreover, change the questions you ask and you will also change your life. You cannot get to somewhere new doing the same things you have always done. If you wish to get different results, you must do different things. Methodically change your patterns of daily life. Change. Move. Shift. Sharpen. Readjust. Press on. REPEAT.

Do you have self-control? Do you have control of your emotions? Do you have control of your desires? Most people will fight change and not take a chance. Most people will choose stability and comfort. Life responds to your assertions and efforts. If you trust your abilities and believe you can have anything you desire. How can you have more than you than you presently have if you don't change your methodology?

You do not have to accept your life as it is. You do not have to accept where you are as your final destination. If you are reading these words, then you can have more. You can have what you want <u>but</u> you have to be willing to change. You can have more than you ever imagined <u>but</u> you cannot remain where you are and doing what you have always have done. Whenever I feel as if things are out of control, I recite aloud The Serenity Prayer: **"God, grant me the serenity to accept the things I cannot change, the courage to change the things I can, and the wisdom to know the difference."** You cannot undo your past in any way but you can disrupt how the past influences your future. You have the power of the present moment. You have control of now.

Do you want the next five years to look like the last five years? If you want the future to look different for you, you need to change your philosophy and habits. If you don't change you will still be exactly where you are right now. Are you holding on to something? You cannot accept what is new if you do not let go of the things you are holding on to. Your present vision and perspective may have you trapped. Inside of you is boundless creativity. Inside of you is infinite imagination. Inside of you is limitless abundance. Re-define and refine your: self. Shift your outlook and you will change your future destination.

> **"Motivation is what gets you started. Habit is what keeps you going"**
>
> **Jim Rohn**

Starts with an idea.
Then an intention.
Then a behavior.

Then a habit.
Then a practice.
Then a second nature.
Then it is simply who you are.

Are you safe? Are you secure? Are you complacent? Being happy and content with what you have and where you are is perfectly acceptable <u>but</u> the successful are NEVER satisfied. Complacency typically expects all of the rewards without the sacrifice. Have you done all you can possibly do? Have you worked as hard as you possibly can? You need to break outside of the box and the barriers that you have placed upon yourself and your life. The successful are always seeking ways to GROW, REFINE and EVOLVE.

"Chains of habit are too light to be felt until they are too heavy to be broken".

Warren Buffett

What are your default responses that will require revision for your success? As socialized beings, we are not trapped in our learning but it is always much easier to continue with bad habits than it is to change them for good ones. We have to continuously self-analyze to know what they are and to be sure not to regress after success. We have to shift our perspective from the short to the long term. We have to be driven to modify our highly routinized lives. Here are some of the most common lazy habits:

Snooze button
Sleep in
Procrastinate
Poor dietary choices
Not reading
Not working out

Break the habits of a lazy routine by motivating yourself to consider your long-term goals. Understand that it is your old ideas and ways that keep you where you are. What good habits can you begin to establish into your daily routine? So much more than you realize is within your control. If you really truly want something, you have to go after it relentlessly.

"The proper work of the mind is the exercise of choice, refusal, yearning, repulsion, preparation, purpose and assent. What then can pollute and clog the mind's proper functioning? Nothing but its own corrupt decisions."

Epictetus

Be the deliberate architect of your life. Every day is your opportunity to build the brilliant you and your brightest future. Good habits are much more difficult to form but easier to live with. Conversely, bad habits are easy to form but challenging to live with. Start now and get into your journal and begin a plan to review your daily schedule and replace bad habits with good habits. You can only accomplish the task at hand today, there is no tomorrow. My son has the bad habit of saying: in five minutes. Five minutes then turns into ten minutes and had he arose at the start; he would have already been done. Be pro-active not passive in your day. Passivity is the gateway to procrastination. Repetition over time will help you to develop good habits but you must make these efforts daily. You create the virtue of discipline through the expression of good lifestyle habits. It takes about twenty-one days to fully initiate a shift in your routine. Remember, lazy doesn't qualify at the racetrack of life and dreams. You must develop your personality and this must happen in every aspect of your life.

"Great acts are made up of small deeds."

Lao Tzu

I have always efforted to develop my personality and lifestyle in such a way there are no veils that exist between my private and public persona. The way that this is accomplished is to engage the smallest tasks with deliberate effort. Effort to engage the few in your life the same way you would engage the many. If you cannot light up a room of three people, how could you even consider influencing three thousand people. If you cannot be mindful of three thousand dollars, how could you consider being the steward of three million dollars. Instead of considering the big steps, consider instead that it is through the continuity and repetition of completing the small tasks deliberately that will become the habits of the best version of you.

Go after it
Be determined
Put in the work
No one is going to hand it to you
Have more faith in yourself
Stay driven
Take all of the necessary steps

The life you want tomorrow demands that you have to take steps toward it today. You cannot receive what you are not reaching for. You know not what you can achieve until you truly immerse your entire being into your work. What if? What could you achieve if you had absolutely no choice? What if your life hung in the balance and you were faced with a life or death circumstance? Viktor R. Frankl, an Austrian Holocaust survivor, psychotherapist and author of the pivotal book "Man's Search for Ultimate Meaning" makes the most profound statement. A perspective that could only be achieved when choice is completely removed from life's equation. He said:

> **"The last of the human freedoms: to choose one's attitude in any given set of circumstances, to choose one's own way. And there were always choices to make. Every day, every hour, offered the opportunity to decide, a decision which determined whether you would or would not submit to those powers which threatened to rob you of your very self, your inner freedom; which determined whether or not you become the plaything to circumstance, renouncing freedom and dignity..."**

Nothing is more powerful than the human spirit. Nothing is more powerful than the will to survive. You have a choice every single moment of the day. What if you had all those options removed? Only a person that has been to the depths of despair. Only a person that has faced life without option. Only a person that has faced certain death and triumphed could possibly summon those words from the ethereal. I urge you to channel your spirit. I urge you to reach deep inside your being. I urge you to find your inner protagonist and fight for your future. Fight for your future as if your life depended on it. I urge you to take control of your destiny. The life and death of your dreams hang in the balance of your decisions. Return to your journal. Regroup and remove everything that is unnecessary from your daily life regimen and REFUSE to give up on your dream.

Are you comfortable? What is your comfort zone? Are you tired? Are you unmotivated? Are you lazy? Are you in a difficult situation? Are you happy? Are you on the path? Take some time to journal about where you are, what you are feeling and how you can change your vantage point. It is important to realize that a positive mindset will not change the circumstance you are currently facing but a positive mindset changes **you**, which ultimately enhances your ability to make the necessary changes to overcome and turn the tides. It is a simple pivot. Make a ninety-degree turn and just look in another direction and now embrace the fresh perspective.

> **"Everyone, at some time or another, sits down to a banquet of consequences."**
>
> **Robert Louis Stevenson**

Success is not a comfortable procedure. Success is somewhat of a torture chamber. Nothing great was ever built without respective effort. In life there will always be times of discomfort, defeat and disappointment; pain is an unavoidable consequence of LIFE. What you need to do is use that pain to get stronger. You need to use that pain to develop your character. You need to use that pain to drive you. You must know the pain, like the clouds in the sky, will always pass. Moreover, there is no greater pain than that of regret.

> **"It is better to act and repent than not to act and regret."**
>
> **Niccolò Machiavelli**

Every time I drive past a cemetery, I wonder how many dreams were taken with those individuals to their graves. How many unwritten books, songs, screenplays, poems...are buried never to manifest? The graveyard is a vast field of buried treasure. Your dreams are either pursued or they <u>will</u> haunt you. Your dreams are <u>never</u> forgotten. Your dreams are calling to you to be chased and attained. Review your journal and write them all down. Are there dreams of your youth that you may have left behind? Are there wishes upon stars that you may have forgotten? Unfulfilled goals will fill your life with anxiety, nervousness and fester inside of you. Unfulfilled goals and desires will constantly drain your energy, while pursuing your dreams will enhance your life force. Passion will increase your energy and drive. Purpose will increase your lifespan. It is in this knowing that should exalt you to be real and dig deep. Remember, that you <u>will</u> reach a point in your life that it <u>will</u> <u>be too late</u>.

"Everyone falls down. Getting back up is how you learn how to walk."

Walt Disney

Sink or Swim? Life will test your fortitude. Instead of passively allowing life to act upon you. Be pro-active and put yourself in uncomfortable situations. Jump in the deep-end and leave yourself no other choice but to succeed. You may swallow some water, but you WILL LIVE. You will fall, but will you get up? You need to get comfortable being uncomfortable if you want to be successful. How mentally tough are you? Do you have the fortitude to deal with anything life throws at you? Are you ready for the fight? A man is no bigger than the smallest thing that provokes him. THINK ABOUT THAT!

You will regret it deeply if you don't build the life you desire. You can pay now or it will COST more later. You need to shift your thoughts from doubt to hope and from believing to knowing. Make hope possessive. Shift from "I hope" to "I have hope". You were made to navigate the road ahead of you. The road ahead may be unknown but that is part of the lesson. You are enough: smart enough, wise enough and strong enough for any of the challenges ahead.

LIFE IS ALWAYS CHANGING…things will NEVER be on an even keel ALL THE TIME. The real challenge of growth comes when you get knocked down. Can you have faith amidst the chaos? How will you handle it? Consider when you are down, it is now that you have an opportunity to rebuild from a solid foundation. It is during these down, dark and sometimes dismal moments where the growth takes place. If you are a hard-working dedicated person, you will not be at the bottom for long!

"I have not failed. I've just found 10,000 ways that won't work."

Thomas A. Edison

Either your troubles/losses/failures make your bitter or they make you better. Don't get bitter, get better. Don't let it hurt, heal and get healthier. Don't get sidetracked, get focused. Don't get peeved, get productive. Do not just go through it, grow through it. Fall, then glow up. Break the chains of the past. Do not let your failures define you, they are your greatest gift. I consider them: divine level-up educators. No one whom has been through tribulation ever remains the same. You typically do not have the ability to choose the <u>out-come</u> but you CAN choose how you <u>come-out</u>; choose growth and evolution every time. The challenge is never the problem, the obstacle is always the answer. Do not allow a hurdle in the race to make you believe the race is over, keep running. When you make a mistake, it is not the end, it is just time to create a new strategy. Let the challenges elevate you. Tie your laces, dig in your heels, pull yourself up by your bootstraps and get ready to rumble for your dreams.

"The only real mistake is the one from which we learn nothing."

Henry Ford

The successful know that it is those failures along the way that serve as guides to your destination. You need to use these moments to not quit but to shift, change and evolve. Successful people override their doubts, fears and challenges in order to rise to excellence. Typically, when you feel the most fear, when you are most scared is the indicator that you are supposed to take-action; it is time to jump. Furthermore, the fear of failure actually pushes the seasoned warrior to work harder to avoid negative outcomes <u>at all costs</u>. Even if success is not met, they NEVER quit. If success is not met, they regroup, refocus and begin again.

You can fear the path or you can have faith in your steps. Both are intangible, both are NOT real, both cannot exist at the same time and you must choose which to believe. Remember, faith is to trust in the future that will only make sense in reverse. Never fear failure but fear being in the same place you are a year from this very moment. You have to know that growth is disruptive. Remember THE SEED, you have to disrupt the ground to plant the seed. You have to know that you cannot have change in your life without disruption.

**When you start to feel the FEAR, dig deep
for your FIRE, feel your passion.
Ask yourself: IF NOT NOW, WHEN?!**

The key to arriving at your goals is to be adaptive. The ability to adapt to change will determine how far you can go. You have to be prepared to change plans. You have to be prepared to alter your strategy. You have to be prepared to adjust your course; knowing all the while that the plan is not as important as <u>the purpose</u>. Review your journal and try to consider your goal from all possible angles. **<u>PIVOT.</u>** You need to know there are countless solutions to every problem if you can free your mind enough to allow them to more easily flow to you and through you. You exist in a world of infinite possibilities and every day you have to adjust your sails to catch the wind in the direction of your desires. The closer you get to your goals, I can guarantee the more intense the world will come at you and that is <u>how I know</u> it is time to <u>RISE</u> to the occasion.

**"The natural healing force within each of us is the
greatest force in getting well."**

Hippocrates

There is always more in you. There is always more to learn. There is always more to practice. There is always more to accomplish. Until your last breath there is always more you CAN do. The ceilings will ultimately become your NEW floors. Difficult is NOT a bad thing, the more challenging the task is, the more value it holds. I always say, if PhD degrees were easy to obtain, everyone would have one. To be quite honest, it was <u>not</u> the most difficult accomplishment of my life <u>but</u> it was a marathon-like endeavor. I will never forget those fourteen years of graduate school. I will never forget that most memorable seventy-two-hour Social Psychology paper mini-marathon devoid of sleep. Anything is possible, as long as you do not allow the trials and tribulations to consume you. I watched so many I started the program with fall away over time because it broke their spirit. Be malleable, just as skyscrapers and bridges are built to flex under stress, you need to also be able to bend and not break. The challenges are to test your resiliency and your respective triumph will always exude pure joy. You will remember for the rest of your life the darkest times you were able to blaze through and forever have pride those accolades.

> **"Winners are not afraid of losing. But losers are. Failure is part of the process of success. People who avoid failure also avoid success."**
>
> **Robert T. Kiyosaki**

Do not take your treasures to the grave. Get back to that list in your journal AGAIN. What are your dreams? What are your goals? What is it that you have inside to gift the world? Poetry, art, science, music, healing, literature, leadership, teaching, coaching, invention, innovation, architecture, love, passion, etc. It is time to identify, improve and increase the viability of those talents you possess and figure out a way to offer them to the planet. IT IS TIME TO GIVE THEM LIFE.

> **"By three methods we may learn wisdom: First, by reflection, which is noblest; Second, by imitation, which is easiest; and third by experience, which is the bitterest."**
>
> **Confucius**

THE HOW: PART III

Do you want to be ordinary?

or

Do you want to be extra-ordinary?

How bad do you want it? Jesse Owens said: **"The road to the Olympics, leads to no city, no country. It goes far beyond New York or Moscow, ancient Greece or Nazi Germany. The road to the Olympics leads — in the end — to the best within us."** The goal for your life should be to be so good at what you do that you cannot be overlooked. A valedictorian will always get their time at the graduation podium. Jesse Owens' words would not have been recorded had he not won the gold medal. Excellence brings visibility and voice. What makes Owens' story even more significant, had he not become a runner his life may have been destined to fulfill the racially biased and **scientifically disproven** "extinction hypothesis" that posited: African Americans were innately / biologically infirmed and were destined for extinction. If it were not for a teacher who saw something special in Owens, I would not have that quote for this paragraph and the world would have not witnessed his greatness. If it were not for the special teachers in my life who saw something in me, I would not be writing this book today. You have the choice every day to fulfill your destiny. You have the choice to disprove EVERYONE! You may even prove something to yourself! How? Do your best in every moment of every day.

You WASTE as many minutes as you complain!

How are you spending these precious moments in time? Stop complaining, figure out who you are, reach for what fires you up and focus on those pursuits with inexorable laser focus. Do not mistake activity for achievement. You can be constantly moving but standing still towards your goals. Do not sit in place and spin your tires. Move and make progress! Keep climbing!

> **"Therefore do not worry about tomorrow, for tomorrow will worry about its own things. Sufficient for the day is its own trouble."**
>
> **Matthew 6:34 NKJV**

I would like you to take a moment to consider the idea that your brain is a computer. Your brain, like a computer has an operating system that has been programmed constantly since the day you were born. You have been inundated with data input and even right now in this moment you are receiving data. As a sociologist, we call this process socialization and there are many programmers in your life that are inputting code to your operating system: family, friends, colleagues and THE MEDIA. You are both a passive and active receptor. It is the time to take control of your firewall and be very deliberate about what algorithms you allow to be written to your hard drive.

Moreover, just like a computer running on an older operating system, you cannot utilize the newest software if you do not update the operating system. If you take the time to meditate on these ideas you will be able to overwrite your current settings and maximize the efficiency of your CPU. The goal is to acknowledge your automatic preset default architecture and defragment your hard drive to get you to your best most effective you and on the fast track to your personal goals. As conditioned beings, we need to be aware that both our actions and reactions to situations have their origins in our history.

Get into your journal, write down the modes below and spend a few moments with each. Take some time to evaluate your feelings and consider how much time every day you spend in these emotional settings.

- Complaining
- Worrying
- Overthinking
- Whining
- Griping
- Stressing
- Anxiety
- Thinking about the past
- Nervousness
- Sadness
- Depression

I am not saying feelings are wrong. Feelings are amazing. Feelings are part of being human. Feelings will be discussed in more depth later. Continuously dig into your memory banks to unearth and modify those negative algorithms. It is important to begin to realize that all of the above have a negative effect on your ability to achieve your goals. Deeply consider why you might be defaulting to these feelings, embrace them and turn towards your better feeling days. Think alchemy and turn that lead into GOLD. Use all of those negative feelings and experiences as fuel to move forward. Use your historical awareness as motivation to never be in that place again.

You will never feel ready to take the leap. The leap of faith will always cost you something. It will cost you what is for what will be. It will cost you the present temporary comfortable couch for the cushioned California king sized bed of your desired future. The pursuit of success is always rife with challenges but I am a living testament to following every single word written in this book.

It may be no surprise with the computer metaphor above that one of my favorite movies of all time is: The Matrix. A few of my best friends say:

The Matrix is a documentary. Early in the film, the main character Neo is placed in a training simulation (The Jump Program) and the goal is to leap across two rooftops. His mentor Morpheus says to him: **"You have to let it all go Neo: fear, doubt and disbelief. Free your mind."** There is surprise among the majority of the group observing when he doesn't succeed having been convinced by Morpheus that he is: The One. The moral of the story, even The One: **"…falls the first time".** You have to make the attempt. Do not look back. Do not go back. Do not hold back. You have to face your fears. You have to jump.

I have many times leapt and flown. Likewise, I have leapt and fallen. I have leapt and broke bones. I have also leapt many times and had my heart broken. I have leapt and had my bank account decimated. I have leapt but every time I have found the grace in the fall. The grace is your opportunity to give it another chance. Every time I have leapt and fell I found the strength to get up and jump again. Jump towards your dreams and you will eventually fly.

Stop running from and start running <u>towards</u> it all. I promise you will never feel ready to face the things that scare you. I promise you will never feel ready to venture into the unknown. You need to feel those feelings, recognize them and let them perish into the ether and take your shot. You need to acknowledge them and then disrupt the negative thoughts with action. Interrupt it, shift it, alchemize it and make your dreams reality.

> **"Experience is not what happens to a man; it is what a man does with what happens to him."**
>
> **Aldous Huxley**

How do you handle tough situations? The majority of us are not going to live as monks separate from the world devoid of the trappings of interpersonal relations, family, work, etc. We do not have the luxury of hours on the mountainside or temple to meditate into the deepest states of Zen. We need to embrace our experiences and trials with stoic stability and serenity. While you cannot avoid stress and disruptions they can be accepted and handled head on. You can attempt to avoid or run from challenges which will ultimately just cause you anxiety and extend those issues further into the future. What I suggest is for you to step into those stressors with a confident mindful steadfast approach to resolve them before they can delay or derail your forward progress.

Worthy of a reprise: the pain of regret is much greater than the pain of failure! You may be a position right now that you are in that in reflection is the result of past unwise decisions. Immaturity, pride, restlessness, fear, lack of information and neglecting forethought will all lead you astray. Life is the ultimate classroom and it is time to PAY ATTENTION! Who could you have been if you started on the path sooner? Where could you be now if you had sharper focus? You <u>do not</u> wish to be in a position later on in life to realize that you did not listen to your innermost voice. Trust me, this will be the most excruciating agony you can imagine as all of your life choices are truly under your control. Ambivalence, indecision and indifference will create more cumulative pain than starting anew into the unknown. Indecision will steal your future opportunities if you do not act. If you are reading this book, regardless of where you are, you are not stuck, YOU STILL HAVE TIME!

> **Therefore I say to you, do not worry about your life, what you will eat or what you will drink; nor about your body, what you will put on. Is not life more than food and the body more than clothing? Look at the birds of the air, for they neither sow nor reap nor gather into barns; yet your heavenly Father feeds them. Are you not of more value than they? Which of you by worrying can add one cubit to his stature?**
>
> **Matthew 6:25-27 NKJV**

Negative emotions simultaneously diminish the quality of the present moment, while moving you away from and further from your goal. Your feelings are valid and valuable. Feel them, heal them and use them. Every high achieving successful individual in the history of the world has had their origins places that were uncomfortable. Success pushes through, rises above and NEVER QUITS. Success gets up one more time than they have been knocked down. It is YOU against YOU and you need to hold yourself accountable. The majority of our internal dialogue is negative and in this final section we will battle the adversary of our own perception of self.

Are you still feeling unworthy of success? Or is it that you are considering the potential discomfort? Life **is** challenging **AND** risky…but…do not let your history predict your limitless potential future. The biggest risk is taking no risk at all. Capture the emotion, capture the wisdom and translate it into equity. All you are and all you have been through has value. Continue to build value in who you are and your history will be your asset; your tests will become part of your testimony.

You must acknowledge yourself. You are free to reinvent yourself at any time, but you must hold yourself accountable for your past. True growth requires acknowledging who you are, where you have been, self-reflection, responsibility and behavioral changes. It is time for you to get in front of the mirror and face yourself. **RIGHT NOW!** Go to a mirror and look at yourself. What do you see? What do you feel about what you see?

Are you doing what you need to be doing to be your best you? Truly acknowledge "you". The you in the mirror is the product of your life choices thus far. Be honest with yourself. Sign a contract with the person in the mirror right now. Completely accept that you are willing to change, that you are willing to transform, that you are willing to "do" what you "need" to do to achieve your goals. What can you change right now? Everything is changeable. There is no aspect of your life that you do not have the power to change.

1N73LLIGE3NCE
15 7H3
4B1L17Y
70 4D4PT 70
CH4NG3

Do not let the habits of your past inhibit you. Focus on what is ahead of you, not behind. Those years behind you were not wasted because you are still here, take the time to re-consider your life as a "classroom" and grab your journal. What have you been taught? What were the lessons? How can you turn the experiences of "your" past into the dividends of your future? Do you wish to be the victim of your life or the victor of your life? Let not your past claim any more of your productive present moment. Use your past as a guide to move forward towards your destiny and no longer as an excuse to remain where you are. Stop right now and refuse to tolerate the place(s) you have settled. It is the time to: **Give yourself a pass from the past. Lift your chin and LOOK UP!** Do not accept that which is beneath you. Do not accept anything less than you deserve. <u>Do believe</u> that your dreams are worth fighting for. Do you accept what life has given you? Have you settled on <u>certain</u> outcomes? Have you settled into <u>certain</u> places? Have you settled with <u>certain</u> people? **<u>NOTHING IS CERTAIN.</u>** Are you willing to refuse to give up? Are you willing to rise to your greatest potential? In order to reach your goals, you have to let go to grow and evolve.

Know: **If you always do what you've always done, then you will always be what you've always been.**

The successful are not superhuman. The successful are normal people who decided they were going to make a change. The successful are normal people who decided they were not going to live ordinary lives. The successful are normal people who decided they were not going to accept their lot. The successful are normal people who decide every single day to push the limits of their reality. You are too <u>that</u> person. You are too <u>that</u> special. You too have greatness inside. You can make that same decision to change. You can challenge the unknown. You can become extra ordinary. How do you do that? It is simple, you simply do it. It is really that simple.

WIN THE MORNING, WIN THE DAY

Win the morning, win the day! Start the day with positive thoughts. The power lies in your mindset. What are your goals again? Do you remember what you wrote earlier? Do you remember your why? What do you really want? Take some time to review your entire book of scribblings. How has your perspective changed? It is time to revise, refine and decide.

> **"Champions don't become champions in the ring – they are merely recognized there. If you want to see where someone develops into a champion, look at his daily routine."**
>
> **John Maxwell**

Today, commit to making the choices that will take you towards your goal. Commit the early part of the day to yourself. Commit the early part of the day to your goals. It is an easier task if we commit the early part of our lives to our goals. Wherever you are in your life, today is the day. No half measures! You have to be fully committed, without full commitment you will never fully make it. Khalil Gibran wrote:

"Do not love half lovers
Do not entertain half friends
Do not indulge in works of the half talented
Do not live half a life
and do not die a half death"

Coaches will tell you that there is an x-factor that exists among the top athletes and that is their intrinsic drive to excel. All of the successful have a relentless drive to be the best they can be. You have to develop a praeternatural drive towards your goals and destiny. Some would argue the fact and say that you cannot decide to be praeternatural, I completely disagree. The Latin origins of the word are in the phrase "praeter naturam", which is translated: beyond nature. You can decide to rise above your nature and strive to push the boundaries of the material world. You can have the world if you can first envision it but you also have to go after it with and unceasing unrelenting unreasonable unrealistic unpractical drive.

Remember, success is taking the small steps every single day. The steps you take do not have to be monumental, they just have to be in the direction of your goal. It is easy to get overwhelmed if we look at the entire staircase; fix your focus on the step that is right in front of you. You are either moving towards your goal, standing still, or moving away from it. Continue to assess your problematic areas that need work.

Continue to assess your routine and default settings that you can reprogram for greater efficiency. Are you a procrastinator? Do you spend more time socially than personally? Do you spend more time working for someone than working on yourself? Do not mistake procrastination for patience; be pro-active! As you take deliberate steps toward your goals you will begin to see that in fact you are more than capable. As you take the steps towards your goals you will be begin to see and feel progress. As you take the steps you will also begin to see small miracles, so pay attention. Be aware of the little surprises during the course of the day. As you take the steps towards your goals you will begin to BELIEVE IT. The small glimpses and epiphanies are the gateway to your dreams. You will notice over time the frequency of tiny miracles will increase and so will your momentum as you deliberately walk each step upward with faith.

To the successful, consistent forward progress is imperative. No movement, procrastination and stagnation are deleterious to your success as it then means you must work double-time to catch up to where you may have been otherwise. Even if you are inching forward, even if you are crawling, you are still making forward progress. You cannot build without a foundation. Maintain a steady gaze forward and any movement is positive if it is in the right direction. Sun Tzu, one of history's greatest military strategists said two-thousand five-hundred years ago: **"Great results, can be achieved with small forces"** and similarly Buddha, a historical purveyor of peace and tranquility stated: **"Think not lightly of good, saying, 'It will not come to me.' Drop by**

drop is the water pot filled. Likewise, the wise man, gathering it little by little, fills himself with good."

You need to take <u>full</u> control of your energies and <u>fully</u> invest in yourself. You need to make the necessary changes to build into your routine the time to focus on your heart, mind and desired future. For example, if you do not take that college course now, it will mean that you have to wait another semester to begin and then it will be even longer before you can finish your curriculum and ultimately earn your degree. Timing is everything. The sooner you begin, the sooner you can be closer to your goals. Yes, I do know that those steps towards the new and unknown are daunting but you must trust that the alternative is even more painful. Yes, I do know that uncertainty is intimidating but the only way to is through. Remember, if your **whys** are strong enough then you will most certainly always figure out a way. We always find time for what we value! We always make time for pleasure! Pledge your time to your future! Make a vow to take the necessary steps upward daily.

Furthermore, be sure to take the time to acknowledge those steps upward and micro-achievements. Celebrating your progress will help to strengthen your self-confidence and resilience as you forge forward to your goals. Take yourself out for a special meal. Get an ice-cream sundae. Buy tickets to a concert. Every Friday night during graduate school, after spending several hours in the library, I would go to the local pub to counter the effects of solitude and reward my efforts. It cannot be all sacrifice and martyrdom; you have to take the time to breathe in life and be human. Life is a balance between the mind, body and spirit; do not renounce your blessings, you were meant to enjoy life. Take some time in your journal to jot down a variety of joyful rewards that you can gift yourself to keep you going.

"It is better to offer no excuse than a bad one."

George Washington

Excuses are the villain in your success story. To neglect your opportunities is to forfeit your future. What are your excuses for not pursuing your dreams? No one is going to give it to you. No one is going to work out for you. No one is going to eat right for you. No one is going to read that book. No one is going to take that course. No one is going to get that degree. No one is going to build that resume. No one is going to apply for that job. No one is going to write that book. No one is going to record that song. No one is going to create that art. No one is going to design that dress for you. No one is going to make sure the work gets done. The only true overseer of your future is you. You are fully responsible for you. You simply have to put in the work. Faith without works is death. If you are reading these words, you have a gift to share with the world and you still have time. No more excuses! No more justifications! No more scapegoats!

"Vision without execution is just hallucination."

Henry Ford

Commit to your goal. Commit to having a productive day. Commit to becoming your best you. Start simply. Start with your body. Start with your routine. Start drinking more water! Hydration, nutrition, and rest are not just about your body, not just about physical wellness, but they are about enhancing your psychic awareness. To be successful, you need to gain complete control of your mind. You cannot be a good student, friend, partner, spouse, employee, entrepreneur, athlete, writer, influencer, etc. if you do not LOVE YOURSELF on all levels! Do you love yourself unconditionally? Head over to the mirror with your journal and look at yourself. Write down all of the things that you love about yourself. You need to embrace all parts of you. You need to embrace every single facet of you. You need to embrace the parts that you hide from the world. The more you love yourself, the easier it is to break those negative habits. Can you love yourself fully? Can you love yourself in the same way you love others? Can you love the seemingly unlovable parts of yourself? Can you love the seemingly damaged parts of you? It is time to unconditionally LOVE YOU!

Your past, your wounds, your scars and your shadows are all what makes you, YOU. The darkest parts of you are what is needed to be embraced the most. Once they are acknowledged and brought to the light you will become not only whole, but you will become an unstoppable force. Once you embrace the whole of you, you will shine brighter; from the inside out. Self-love is essential, especially in American/Western culture that promotes at every angle a self-loathing and self-hatred. Embrace the unique that is you. Embrace the fact that no one is you and that is your super power. Do you want to be one of the sheep or the shepherd? Your life is not just a gift, it is <u>your</u> gift that you bring to the world and that is <u>your why</u>. **It is your time.** It is up to <u>you</u> to start to unwrap and embrace each precious new day you are given.

One of the greatest illusions in life: Shortcuts

Get up one hour earlier than usual. Get right up, no snooze button! It takes time to build a new routine. Physiologically your body will not enjoy a new sleep pattern immediately but trust that it will adjust. You may try to go to bed earlier to start to shift your body's internal clock. Consider if you get a little less sleep it means that you will be able to complete one more task. Trust me, when you have accomplished all you can for the day, you will be more relaxed, rest even easier and more soundly.

You need a vision, you need a goal, you need a dream to pursue and the time is now. However, your time to achieve your goals is constantly slipping through the hourglass. Fact: most billionaires wake up at four in the morning! They actually find that it is their most productive time of the day. Wayne Dyer said many times that his time to write was at 3AM. If you can start to look at your future as something to look forward to, you will wake up. Trust me, once you find your purpose you will be so motivated that you will not even NEED to set the alarm. Your passion and drive will become your wake-up call. The greatness inside of you is just waiting for you to flip the switch and once you do, nothing in this world will be able to stop you. You will always find time for what is important. Greatness embodied is to overcome your limitations and you will know it when you surprise even yourself. Greatness is discovered in the process. The gauntlet to your goal is arduous and tedious but there are no shortcuts; endurance is vital. Handle your difficult times with care until they become good times.

Rise and Grind. Get up and greet the "new" day. In addition to your earlier alarm setting, another part of your new regimen is to integrate positivity into your day, every day. Begin each day by saying THANK YOU. To say thank you in advance for what already yours, to give thanks for what is on its way to you, and to say thank you for the amazing opportunities that are coming your way today.

When you open your eyes be thankful for another day to pursue your dreams. I am thankful for:

- Breath
- Love
- Grace
- Kindness
- Prosperity
- Life

Positive affirmations at the start of each day will set your personal GPS in the right direction towards your best destiny. Over time, not only will this be an automatic process for you but you will find that all of the universe will conspire to bring all that goodness on to your path.

> **"See then that you walk circumspectly, not as fools but as wise, redeeming the time, because the days are evil."**
>
> **Ephesians 5:15-16**

Every morning when you wake up, you are living moments you will never live again. Every morning when you wake up, you are breathing air you will never breathe again. Every morning when you wake up is the chance to realize that it is a new day that you have never lived before. Every morning when you wake up is another opportunity to make this day even better than the last. What you do with this day is up to you and again time is your most precious commodity and nonrenewable resource. You are powerful. You have the power to set the tone for your day. It is called the present for a reason; will you use this gift wisely or will you let it slip away into the ethers.

The Best in the World. Do you desire to become the best in the world? Do you wish to become a master in a discipline? It all starts from where you are right now. Every blackbelt in martial arts began with their white belt. You need to accept and embrace where you are right now. You need to find humility in your position in the hierarchy as those above you are there for a reason. You cannot expect to be blessed with the gifts of the world if you cannot be faithful over the small things in your life. Whatever is currently expected of you needs to be approached with the utmost deliberate care for you to be offered more. If you can not be committed to the few you will not be granted the gifts of the many. You may want more money but can you balance your current budget? You may want a house but can you take care of your apartment? Another secret to success is having a consistent desire to acquire wisdom from every moment, at every stage along your journey; there is always something to learn from every person you meet. Be sincere. Be receptive. Be humble.

> **"The man who does more than he is paid for will soon be paid for more than he does."**
>
> **Napoleon Hill**

My success in life has stemmed from two general principles: accepting whatever opportunity that was presented to me <u>and</u> simply doing my absolute best wherever I was at that moment. When I was in my senior year of high school, I worked at a famous sandwich franchise. I didn't enjoy that job but I made the best sandwiches I could for every single customer. It became evident as many customers started to request that their food pass through my hands. It did not take much time, within the span of two months I was promoted to manager and possessed a key to the store. While I was happy and grateful to be making sandwiches, I also knew that I needed to be working simultaneously on my studies and also my passion project in music. I did not wish to be making subs forever but I knew if I desired I could open a franchise. The moral of the story: you have to be fully immersed and dedicated where you are but also active, open and receptive to the next places you may be called to go.

"Once you understand the way broadly, you can see it in all things"

Miyamoto Musashi

If you desire to "be" prosperous than you must "be" above average. Musashi urges us to consider integrating excellence into all that we do. All of the while, you <u>will</u> have struggles, you will have circumstances and whether or not you are prepared for them, you STILL have to push through them to get to the next level. You have to always prepare excellently and then you always know that your best, regardless of outcome, is always enough. Those are the circumstances that test your faith and desire, do you WANT it enough to get over that speed bump, that rough path, that lost battle; THIS "is" the process. Wisdom is gained during the process. Tomorrow. If you are lucky enough to get another tomorrow, use your compounding wisdom to maximize the value of every day.

"The secret to success is to do the common things uncommonly well."

John D. Rockefeller

Jim Rohn stressed the idea: just because you are working for someone else does not mean you cannot work on yourself. Take every opportunity to enhance your resume. Take every opportunity to consider your current environment to maximize your present moment. Take every opportunity to build technical competence in your desired field. Take every opportunity to enhance life skills daily. Take every opportunity to notice what options may be available that are aligned with your goals. Know that a breakthrough can happen at any moment. Know that even the smallest interaction might contribute to a massive future outcome.

You cannot simply be "good" at something, you have to be "phenomenal" at something to reach your dream destination. All you have to do is follow a very *simple* logical progression. First, you need to begin because dreams and goals without action are just a sure path to delusion and depression. Second, you need to harness the will to push past beginner. Third, is to continue to work, sharpen your skills and push past mediocre to good. Finally, continue to push past great until you are a master expert. Success is built, not bought. Success is earned, not given. Success is the outcome of hard work, not easy. Success is rare, not average.

Napoleon Hill wrote: **"The ladder of success is never crowded at the top"**. Complementarily, eight-time Olympic gold medalist Usain Bolt said: **"I trained 4 years to run 9 seconds, and people give up when they don't see results in 2 months." Reread those quotes. Write them in your journal.** Let those notions just sink in. How truly committed are you? How truly dedicated are you? How much desire do you possess for the desired outcome? Structure your life and ritual habits with the goal to be the best you possible and you might find that you are one day the best in the world. Even if you fall short, at minimal you can be among the elite in your field.

> **"Death and life are in the power of the tongue, And those who love it will eat its fruit."**
>
> **Proverbs 18:21 NKJV**

You will fall. You will fail. When you are down, when you are at your lowest, it is very easy to stay in those dark, low places; I promise that you will find no lack of company in that pit of despair. I also promise you, that if you can find the strength to crawl out of the pit and back onto the path it will be simultaneously the most painful and beautiful experience you will ever have in your life. Achievement somehow makes all of the pain and struggle instantly disappear. To return to a previous analogy, when you fall or are pushed into a dark place, you are never there to be buried; know in your heart you have been planted. Use that time to re-evaluate, to re-build and to get ready to rise **again**. Where you are is where you are supposed to be and the point once again it is not a place you ever HAVE TO STAY. You are NEVER given anything in life that you CANNOT handle and there is NO-THING that is TOO MUCH because YOU are always ENOUGH and YOU CAN DO IT!

Subatomic Manifestation and Manipulation

> **"Ask, and it will be given to you; seek, and you will find; knock, and it will be opened to you. For everyone who asks receives, and he who seeks finds, and to him who knocks it will be opened."**
>
> **Matthew 7:7-8 NKJV**

I am sure that you have heard a magician utter the word: Abracadabra. Abracadabra is a Hebrew word, and its translation into English is: "I create as I speak". What are you speaking into existence? What are you saying when you are down? What are you saying while you are in the fight? You have to be not only active in the pursuit of your goals but pro-active in both your thoughts and the words that come out of your mouth. Thoughts become things and your words are even more powerful.

All is matter! You are matter!! You matter!!! It all matters!!!!

Scientific research continues to support these concepts through quantum theory such that reality is both what we *choose* to see and what we choose to think. Obviously, these are incredibly complex theories but there is a simplicity at the conceptual level. The general notion is to embrace the fact that you are a deliberate creator and active participant in your ultimate reality. Our reality depends on where we focus, what we assert, the world then responds and we continuously repeat that process. Relatedly, in my sociology courses, I discuss the nature of questions: if you want something you have to "ask" and the worst possible response to the request is: no. You can never have what you do not ask for. Conversely, you will never know the answer unless you ask the question. If you just think about what you want without asking or taking action, that is dreaming or delusion. Moreover, what is amazing is YOU NEVER HAVE TO ACCEPT the answer, you can just as JK Rowling did; continue on down the hallway and continue to knock on doors until you receive the answer you desire.

Choices and decisions always have consequences. We cannot control the outcomes but we have control over both our responses and re-actions to that respective feedback. You can and should look back (**but do not stay there too long**) at your life and you will find that you are a product of every word you have spoken. You are a product of every conversation and interaction you have ever had in your entire life. You are the culmination of every decision or passive acceptance you have made up until this very moment in your life. Take some time in your journal to reflect on the significant choices and events that have led to this point in your life. As well, consider the decisions that you did not actively choose. Sometimes we allow others to make decisions for us by following their lead. How many times in your life were you the supporting actor in someone else's story?

To be successful you must understand the power of presence but also that of the subconscious mind. Why are you not where you wish to be? The answer might be that you are actively inhibiting your own progress subconsciously. Get back to your journal and ask yourself the very serious question: What am I doing right now to derail my achievements? How might I be self-sabotaging my success? What things come to mind when you muse your relationship to your goals and the underlying thoughts about where you are and where you wish to be? Anything is possible but you have to get to the root of it all and build your new life on a firm foundation.

To get to a new place you must be incredibly deliberate and every part of the process is important; everything matters. To get to your desired destination, you need to learn <u>how</u> to speak to not <u>what</u> is happening, but your focus needs to be forward. You need to focus on the <u>where</u> you want to be, the what you want to be, the <u>who</u> you want to be, to arrive at the who you ARE in your imagination. The key is to believe in your future, to be able to feel your future with your senses before it even happens. As you begin to consistently think in terms of your future goals and possibilities, you <u>will</u> actually create new patterns in your brain and you <u>will</u> become a magnet for everything you desire.

Set your dream GPS and the world will shift around you. Emotionally embrace and feel your success as if it were here right now. Tony Robbins speaks to the power of the Reticular Activating System (RAS), which is the bundle of nerves at the base of the brain stem. The RAS is a life experience filter that assists the subconscious to more easily reveal the direct path to your goal. For example, you are in the market for a particular car and as you begin your process towards purchasing the new vehicle, you seem to see <u>more</u> of those cars on the road. It is not that there are more, but your brain is actively seeking those cars and they are part of your driven focus, pun intended. Athletes call this level of concentration and laser focus: being in the ZONE. As well, you can think of the RAS as an architect that will give your mind the blueprints to build whatever you desire into your life. Change your thoughts, change your life. Over time, as your perspective shifts, your focus will begin to acutely hone in on your goals and your mind will automatically filter out the unnecessary static and distractions. As you learn to tap into the power of your mind, like bolts of lightning: new ideas will arise, significant breakthroughs appear and opportunities will seemingly just fall into your lap.

We discussed earlier the importance of writing your down your goals but now I want you to go back to your journal and re-write them again with intention. As you write each goal, create a mental image of <u>you</u> actually achieving those desired outcomes. The process of combining visualization and kinesthetics will firmly imprint those goals into your supercomputer brain. Joe Dispenza has focused a great deal of his work on the ability of us to rewire our brains. He now has the data to support the power of our thoughts to influence our reality. Neuroscientific research has solidified that consistent focus on singular intentioned concepts and ideas will facilitate physical changes in the brain. Furthermore, new learning and experiences will actually initiate the growth of new neurons and trigger genetic evolution. We now have proof that you have the ability to morph your entire being from the inside out. You have the ability to manipulate your genetic code. You have the ability to hack The Matrix and the key to your personal (re-)evolution lies in <u>your</u> thoughts, <u>your</u> hands, <u>your</u> regimen, <u>your</u> actions, <u>your</u> resolute determination and <u>your</u> limitless imagination.

Success comes in cans, not in cannots.

There are hundreds of books that discuss mind over matter and the power of positive thought. Norman Vincent Peale titled his classic text and a must read: The Power of Positive Thinking. A couple of standout tenets asserted by Peale in this revolutionary book are: **"Expect the best and get it** and **Believe in yourself and in everything you do."** I would like you to now consider these two statements: **Do you think you can't** or **Do you think you will**; they are actually both correct. Which one do you choose to believe? The power of positive thinking isn't pretending that everything <u>is</u> good. Everything is not always good. Everything is not always happy. Everything is not always joyous. However, there is something to learn in everything you experience. The power of positive thinking is the ability to see the good in everything. The power of positive thinking isn't pretending that you have what you want. The power of positive thinking is to believe you can have what you want.

The power of positive thinking is the ability to truly <u>feel</u> that you have acquired the desired goal. If you want a car, you must actually be able to see and feel yourself in that vehicle, driving it, possessing it and seeing it in your driveway. Can you feel yourself holding the keys in your hands? Can you feel yourself driving that vehicle? Can you feel the wind in your hair? The best athletes use this type of visualization technique; they will imagine their performance and they will feel it as if it happened in their mind and body. Jack Nicklaus, a hall-of-fame golfer utilized detailed imagery to enhance his focus and performance. He stated:

"I never hit a shot, not even in practice, without having a very sharp, in-focus picture of it in my head. It's like a color movie. First, I see the ball where I want it to finish, nice and white and sitting up high on the bright green grass. Then, the scene quickly changes, and I see the ball going there: its path, trajectory, and shape, even its behavior on landing. Then there is a sort of fade-out, and the next scene shows me making the kind of swing that will turn the previous images into reality."

Wayne Gretzky, a hall-of-fame hockey player also notes using this type of visualization technique. He recalls:

"We taped a lot of pictures on the locker room door: Bobby Orr, Potvin, Beliveau, all holding the Stanley Cup. We'd stand back and look at them and envision ourselves doing it. I really believe if you visualize yourself doing something, you can make that image come true ... I must have rehearsed it ten thousand times. And when it came true it was like an electric bolt went up my spine."

Sports psychology research has scientific support for these visualization techniques; it is called: functional equivalence. Generally, we can consider that there is a similarity between the brain activities of mental practice and that of physical activity. Functional equivalence posits that when physical action is visualized, you actually stimulate the same muscles that would be used to complete the action. Similarly, the bodybuilding icon, actor and politician Arnold Schwarzenegger had a very distinct image in his mind of who he wished to become which paved the path for his profound physical metamorphosis. He said:

"I had this fixed idea of growing a body like Reg Park's. The model was there in my mind; I only had to grow enough to fill it. The more I focused in on this image and worked and grew, the more I saw it was real and possible for me to be like him. What you do is create a vision of who you want to be — and then live that picture as if it were already true."

All of these techniques take deliberate and distinct practice. The purpose of this book is to give you as many inspirational ideas and techniques to assist you in harnessing the power to achieve your goals. Each of us are unique individuals and you will eventually gravitate towards a practice that suits your way of being. Practice does not make perfect. Consistent practice is essential. Consistency establishes patterns, muscle memory and growth. Continuous practice makes permanence. Be sure to always do what you do "on purpose" and "with purpose". Perfection comes with time and dedication. Bruce Lee once said: I fear not the man who has practiced 10,000 kicks once, but I fear the man who has practiced one kick 10,000 times. As you will begin to see, all of these seemingly different paths and techniques are all facets of the same diamond and **how** you wish to see your world.

The Origin of Humanness

I begin and end my introduction to sociology course with a nod to philosophy. Taking time to muse the origins of who we are and how we came to be who we are is a most worthy endeavor. It is a powerful exercise to examine deeply what it means to be human. I believe we all crave to understand life's meaning in some way; especially during the challenging times. Write in your journal the words: Who am I? Take a few moments and consider who you are beneath it all. The French philosopher Rene Descartes takes us deeper with his famous words first written in 1637: Je pense, donc je suis / Cogito ergo sum / I think therefore I am. Take some time to not only consider who you are but to also critically assess your thoughts and questions about your relationship to the external world. Descartes logic posits that it is our ability to question our existence which ultimately supports the hypothesis that we actually do exist. If we question then we must think, therefore, reading this book and evaluating these ideas confirms that you exist; at least as a thinking being.

Socrates urges us to push beyond our lived experience with his paradox: I only know that I don't know. What do we really know? Sociologically, I assert to my students that we only know through our own eyes and our lived experience. However, the poem by John Godfrey Saxe, which is based on a Hindu parable prompts us to question that experiential angle of the world at which we are facing and are feeling. You need to realize and humble yourself enough to accept you are not omniscient. You need to realize that you are limited by your partial understanding of the world. You need to realize that you see the world through your distinct value-laden perspective.

> **It was six men of Indostan, to learning much inclined, who went to see the elephant (Though all of them were blind), that each by observation, might satisfy his mind.**

> **The first approached the elephant, and, happening to fall, against his broad and sturdy side, at once began to bawl: "God bless me! but the elephant, is nothing but a wall!"**

> **The second feeling of the tusk, cried: "Ho! what have we here, so very round and smooth and sharp? To me tis mighty clear, this wonder of an elephant, is very like a spear!"**

> **The third approached the animal, and, happening to take, the squirming trunk within his hands, "I see," quoth he, the elephant is very like a snake!"**

> **The fourth reached out his eager hand, and felt about the knee: "What most this wondrous beast is like, is mighty plain," quoth he; "Tis clear enough the elephant is very like a tree."**

> **The fifth, who chanced to touch the ear, Said; "E'en the blindest man can tell what this resembles most;**

Deny the fact who can, This marvel of an elephant, is very like a fan!"

The sixth no sooner had begun, about the beast to grope, than, seizing on the swinging tail, that fell within his scope, "I see," quothe he, "the elephant is very like a rope!"

And so these men of Indostan, disputed loud and long, each in his own opinion, exceeding stiff and strong, Though each was partly in the right, and all were in the wrong!

So, oft in theologic wars, the disputants, I ween, tread on in utter ignorance, of what each other mean, and prate about the elephant, not one of them has seen!

Ironically, it is only someone who is not blind can understand what is happening in the above scenario. Just as NEO in THE MATRIX movie could not be told but shown what "it" actually was, you must begin to evaluate your perspectives. Most of the time we are acting in the world with incomplete information. Most of the time we are acting and reacting based on our biases, beliefs and distortions of our perception of reality.

As previously discussed, as it is important to get to the core of your-self and discover what you really truly desire. Philosophy brings us to the core of our existence and assists us by removing us from the confines of our social selves to consider the essence of pure consciousness.

The philosophical and socio-psychological rabbit holes of internal discovery are infinite. Once you begin to consider your existence, your thoughts may shift to sensation, perception and evolution. As an academic, I appreciate the variety of theoretical facets that endeavor to explain how we are in the world. So many different ideas abound to rationalize what propelled us as humans into this present future as we know it. I personally enjoy delving into the deepest reaches of our subconscious, detangling the connection of our past experiences that have unconsciously shaped our present reality. To examine the depths of the mind may be the key to your own personal breakthrough that is necessary to open the floodgate to your greatest achievements. Countless models of Human Development exist and they each have their utility, unique perspective and in my less than exhaustive list those marked with asterisk are my personal favorites.

Atmananda's Model of Spiritual Development

Bandura's Social Learning Theory

Brofenbrenner's Bioecological Model of Human Development

Freud's Theory of Psychosexual Development

Darwin's Theory of Evolution

Gebser's Structures of Human Consciousness

Graves's Spiral Dynamics (SD) Model

Hawkins's Scientific Model*

Jung's Theories of Archetypes and The Collective Unconscious*

Hurtak's Model of Spiritual Development

Kegan's Model of Psychological Development

Kohlberg's Model of Moral Development

Loevinger's Model of Ego-state Development

Maslow's Hierarchy of Needs*

McTaggart's Scientific Model

May's Model of Development of Consciousness

Myss's Model of Spiritual Development

Perry's Model of Intellectual and Ethical Development

Piaget's Model of Cognitive Development

Pribam's Scientific Model

Tolle's Model of Spiritual Development

Vygotsky's Sociocultural Theory of Cognitive Development

Wilber's AQAL Model

Emotional Guidance: The Law of Attraction and Energy

Pay very close attention to your feelings. Your feelings are your guides. Use your feelings to navigate during the course of your day. Negative affect in the form of emotional, mental, physical and/or financial turbulence are guides that let you know you are <u>NOT</u> in the right place. You have to learn to feel into life. You have to learn to trust your instincts. You have to learn to trust your intuition. You have to learn to trust and lean into your feelings as they are your life course GPS. As Rumi and others have said: **silence gives answers.**

Many people assume that if they think happy thoughts that they will somehow be happier. We cannot and should not <u>avoid</u> our emotions and thoughts. Emotional bypassing, spiritual bypassing and toxic positivity are endemic in the self-help community. It is imperative to acknowledge fully our negative emotions: sadness, anger, fear, doubt, etc. The negative can and will <u>always</u> lead you to the good if you have the courage and fortitude to climb the ladder.

You must learn to take inventory of your feelings and let's integrate a popular term into conversation: trending. Where are you trending? Are you trending in the direction of love or fear? See the image below and note that they are on opposite ends of the spiral. The law of attraction posits that you will magnetize what field you are fixated in; your vibe attracts your tribe. You really have to take your feelings and thoughts seriously.

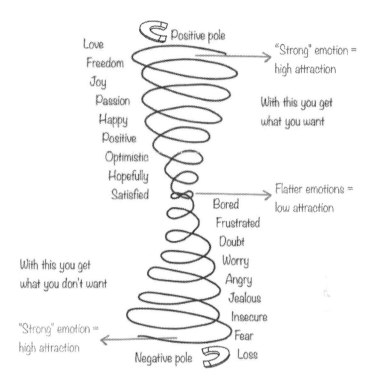

The law of attraction school posits: it is okay to <u>feel</u> lower on the scale emotions <u>but</u> you have to do your best to not start trending in the lower vibrations. Even those in the counseling fields will tell you to embrace your feelings, greet them, to understand the reason for their presence and then send them off; thank them for their visit. Don't stay down there! Do not stay fixed on "what is"…focus on where you want to be. The longer you dwell in the lower parts of the scale, you will sink further down and draw in more of the same; misery indeed loves company. It helps to look at the illustration to reflect where you <u>are</u> emotionally and where you have to then **go** to get where you <u>need to be</u>. The most effective reset for me is a meditative nap. If I find myself in a challenging state or have reached the limit to my productivity, I will carve out a fifteen to forty-five-minute nap to reset. Ninety-nine percent of the time I will emerge much higher on the scale. Another technique is to shift your focus to other areas in your life and surroundings you can appreciate…and then use those to boost you upward emotionally to where you need to be. Trust me, it takes a **<u>LOT</u>** of practice.

You must learn to pay close attention to the world around you. There is an interconnected nature of things and the more you are aligned with your life's purpose you will begin to see and feel unexplainable forces that will guide you along your way. Carl Jung called these experiences: synchronicities. It is a choice for how you will look at the world. Do you look at things as just random disconnected occurrences? Jung and others like Dolores Cannon believe there is a deeper layer of divine orchestration if you actively <u>choose to</u> observe.

The life you live has everything to do with the way you focus your attention. If you focus on what is wrong then you will attract more worry and fear. If you focus on gratitude then you will attract more to appreciate and love. You will always get what you focus on. Ironically, if you focus on things you do not want, you will get more of those things you do not desire. <u>Where</u> you focus your thoughts <u>will</u> direct the compass of your day. You must be a deliberate creator, keep your wits about you and know that thoughts become things.

Intuition is your connection to your inner guide and higher self. Prayer is the request and intuition is the answer. Intuition is sometimes a slight whisper or a deep resonant urge that offers direction and insight that are beyond your conscious understanding. You need to learn to trust these hunches and begin to believe that they are indeed significant spiritual communications. Meditation can assist in the quieting of the noise of the outside world and your inner chatter to get to the essence of your being. I am a huge admirer of the definitive Florence Scoville Shinn and her contemporary Esther Hicks. As with everything written in this book, you are always presented with a choice: are these just random feelings we feel or are they your divine insights that have the potential to lead you to the most extraordinary events and miraculous outcomes; I always choose the latter.

Your vibe attracts your tribe. I have found that when I am feeling physically or emotionally depleted in a particular place or in the presence of a person or people, there is something potentially wrong there that deserves attention. For example, there was a business I used to frequent and I would have a profound anxiety while visiting. I could not figure out the reason why but knew something was off and I would leave feeling very depleted. Ignoring what was in retrospect right in front of me, I still questioned myself. I thought perhaps I was coming down with a cold, I needed more sleep or attributing it to other things that were happening in my life; not once considering it was the environment. Luke 8:17 conveys: **"For nothing is secret that will not be revealed, nor anything hidden that will not be known and come to light" (NKJV).** Ultimately, I came to find out several weeks later in a conversation with a mutual friend that the owner and a few employees (all of which I had considered friends) used to talk very negatively about me behind my back. Feelings, vibes, energy or whatever term you wish to use doesn't lie. Trust your gut, trust your intuition and <u>trust that it is never wrong</u>. In my case, those feelings were the indicators that I was NOT in the RIGHT place.

As well, negative feelings, can be interpreted that you are straying further from where you should be on your path. If you are not in alignment, you will know you're not on your path, your inner-guides will urge you to take immediate action. Be aware and be vigilant, if that happens to be the case and you do not act and you do not make the necessary changes you will find these negative experiences and emotions will continue to increase exponentially. Use the power of discernment to figure out the reason for your discomfort. Anytime your soul feels anxious, it is a not-so-subtle sign to move. Do not betray yourself by staying in places that no longer serve you. As you learn to tune into your emotions, you will find that if anything, any place, any person or any situation that is not in alignment with your purpose will incite emotional warnings.

> **"Be civil to all; sociable to many; familiar with few; friend to one; enemy to none."**
>
> **Benjamin Franklin**

Finally, there is the loveliest of quantum notions is that we "entangle" with another observer when we communicate. I say lovely, because I have and continue to be blessed with an amazing circle of people in my world that share my vision, share my love and we mutually support our endeavors; and we just vibe. How do you know who they are? You will just know. You will know to your core who your people are. You will know not only by how you feel in their presence but you will have an uncanny mutual understanding between you. Moreover, you need to take very seriously and carefully consider with whom you not only allow into your network but whom you intimately enmesh your energy and life with. The law of constructive interference posits when two waves of the same wavelength frequency interact and align, a new wave will be created that is larger than the original wave. Take a moment to get into your journal and list the people you closely interact with on a regular basis. Reflect on your relationships and try to document how you felt the last time you were with those individuals. Did you feel invigorated or drained? What were the topics of conversation? What were the activities that you engaged? You can increase your energy by aligning with people of like frequency or they can actually detract from you and lower your vibration. Choose your interactions and associations wisely.

> **"They went out from us, but they were not of us; for if they had been of us, they would have continued with us; but they went out that they might be made manifest, that none of them were of us."**
>
> **1 John 2:19 NKJV**

Do you have enemies? Good, that means you are doing something meaningful. It is important to be aware that if we wish to reach our highest goals that we cannot do it alone. Extreme self-reliance can become self-sabotage but do choose the right teammates. Never forget, it is critical that we be careful and deliberate with whom we associate. Have you ever heard the saying: **loose lips sink ships**? Additionally, you even have to be mindful of who you share your innermost feelings, thoughts, desires, dreams and especially your future plans. If you look closely at the people in your life, you will see your future. Perhaps in your present evaluation of your associations you might be inclined to be a more <u>active</u> participant in <u>your</u> life. As you begin to take seriously your social network, you will begin to take seriously who is privy to your innermost depths, desires and dreams.

> **"Just because they ride with you, doesn't mean they ride for you."**
>
> **Urban American Proverb**

In retrospect, I can see quite clearly the mistakes I made in trusting the "wrong" people. Understand, they were not necessarily wrong or bad people but I did not take the time to realize they were merely acquaintances rather than true friends. Admiration does not imply ALLEGIANCE. If you pay close attention, you may not have to pay the high price of hindsight. Do they truly <u>listen</u> when you share bad news? "Your people" are <u>always</u> in support of you and will always listen. "Your people" will never waver. You will never have to worry about your safety when you are in the presence of "your people". Take a moment to think, when all falls away will they be standing with you or someone else. A friend loves at all times. When you have good news do they help you celebrate? "Your people" will be there fully both at the bottom and the top of your journey. **Pause, watch, look and listen.** How do they talk about other people? If they speak negatively about others, it is likely they will do the same when not in your presence. If you share something with them, can you trust that they will not only support you but will they keep your secrets; not everyone is trustworthy. So, who is worthy of your trust? As noted above, use your intuition and you will <u>know</u> in your heart and soul who these people are. Your people: they are your ride or die people, they are your through thick and thin friends, they are your drive to airport at three in the morning people and you can always trust their absolute transparency and honesty. Everyone is a teacher, even your enemies. Shift your perspective and view those ill-intentioned associates as: beneficial adversaries.

> **"Your enemies can kill you, but only your friends can hurt you."**
>
> **Marcus Tullius Cicero**

Your real people may hurt your feelings but you need to step out of your ego and evaluate the source. You need to differentiate if what was said was in your best interest or in opposition to your deepest desires and dreams? A true friend will tell you like it is because they care about you. A beneficial adversary will tell you something because they might be jealous of your progress. A tell-tale sign of the fair-weather association is to reflect on and begin to pay close attention to their reactions to what is happening in your life. Are they there when you are struggling? Do they check in on you periodically? Are they supportive or supporting your battle? Are they on the side of what is good for you? Are they happy when you are winning or are they becoming distant? Are they celebrating with you or for you? If you look closely, you will see that some people are there just for the party. Those who are not truly in support of you and will come for the food and leave. Who is there early? Who stays when it is over to clean up? Who has been around through the good times and the bad? Even your closest family members may disappear from your life when the tides shift and you are no longer of value to them. People tend to leave your life when you no longer serve a mutual cause. As stated earlier, misery loves company and sometimes people are interested in associating with others whom are at their level or below. When you tell them bad news are they supportive? Do they find ways to offer you assistance? Are they grieving when you are? Does the phone ring for a connection or only for a favor? Be honest with yourself. Review your closest ten "friends" and if all you had to offer was your <u>friendship</u>, who would still remain in your circle? Choose people who are your biggest supporters on your path to success and are also your softest landing when you fall down. Your friends should possess these fundamental traits: supporting, trustworthy, honest, empathic and LOVING.

> **"A wise man gets more use from his enemies than a fool from his friends."**
>
> **Baltasar Gracian**

It is important to be trusting but simultaneously you have to be aware there is always the potential for betrayal. At some point in your life, you will have made the mistake of thinking someone was for you but you must realize that that even the good were not meant to stay. When someone shows you who they are: believe them. Remember if, every relationship we have in our life has a purpose to teach us something about life; every person a teacher. Every relationship we have in our life is either a blessing or a lesson. Embrace that even the lesson is a blessing and the silver lining outcome is WISDOM.

Understand that most people that come into our lives are not to be there forever and the same is true for members of our immediate biological family. Time will always reveal those who are fully in support of you or just temporary actors and extras in the closing credits of your life story. Remember, time is way too valuable to spend with people who are not one-hundred percent in support of you. But even if you are a victim in one scene you must continue forth to be the victor in the end. You have the ability to write the script and cast for the roles in your story. Ultimately, it is not the size of your circle but the loyalty and quality of the people in it that matters most. You have to actively defend at every turn your light and your dreams with your life.

> **"Even the finest sword plunged into salt water will eventually rust."**
>
> **Sun Tzu**

As you begin to be protective of your energy and your finite resources, those who remain are your true friends and family. As you take control of your life, as you begin to evolve, as you raise your vibration you will notice that your entire social network will shift. You will begin to rise and soar like the eagle and only other eagles will be able to handle the altitude. So, do not fear as your intimate circle too begins to evolve. Do not fear this likely solitary transitional period in the wilderness. As well, the assistance you may need might not arrive in the form of a familiar face. Stay true to yourself, do not look back, do not go back…keep your eyes fixed forward. You will eventually begin to attract people who will help you cultivate the seeds of your destiny. You will begin to attract those who truly appreciate your unique gifts and provide you with the necessary unconditional approval and support. You will begin to attract people who will both nourish and inspire you. You want people close who want the best for you not just the best parts of you. Iron sharpens iron. Ironically, that may not be a familiar face but the next stranger you meet and when you least expect it. Be aware and be open.

> **"Great minds discuss ideas; average minds discuss events; small minds discuss people."**
>
> **Eleanor Roosevelt**

Show me your friends and I will show you your future. Mike Tyson said "if you are a friend to everybody, you are an enemy to yourself." You need to get real about your associations and connections. Seriously assess and determine if your current relationships are moving you in the direction of your goals. One of the biggest factors that can inhibit your evolution and growth: relationships that no longer have value. You will outgrow people and you must know that your future will not include everyone from your past. I heard someone say: take a serious look at the people in your circle and if you do not get inspired, you don't have a circle you have a cage! Change your surroundings, change your mind, change your perspective and you will change your life.

> You should not be in places that do not bring value to your life
> You should not associate with people who
> do not bring value to your life
> You should not make purchases that do not bring value into your life

It is time for you to upgrade. As you begin to work on yourself, you want to meditate and focus on the people you want to attract in your life. Do you associate with people who are "not" motivated? Separate yourself from friends who do not have goals or dreams. Do you associate with intelligent, savvy and critical thinking people? You need to align with people that you can learn from, be inspired by and will push your limits. Are you connected with people who drain your energy? Stay away from people who are consistently troubled, unhappy, blame others, intoxicated or addicted to alcohol and drugs. It is necessary to align yourself with the dreamers, the strivers, the doers, the hungry! If you want to live your dream, consider not just the people but also be weary of the "rooms" you enter. Where are you spending your time? Look around, if you are the smartest person in the room then perhaps you are in the wrong room. An MIT study noted that you are likely to earn within $2-3K of your closest friends. Start today and assess your tribe. Whatever the life you wish to create, you need to consistently cultivate the most solid social network you can assemble.

Be active in the process. It is better to be in solitude than to spend time and energy with people that will deter you from your goals. You need to be selective of whom you spend your precious time with. Are you the leader in your group? Are you the most intelligent person in your group? Are you the wealthiest person in the group? What is it that you talk about with your people? Do you discuss the past, present or future? Are they interested in growth and evolution? Go through your recent text messages, emails and phone calls to see who is truly there for you? What was the content of those conversations? What are their goals and current projects? Do they hold you accountable? Are they fixated on excellence? How supportive are they of your goals? You have to be gravely serious about your time. How many years do we actually have in this life? How much time do you have left? How much time have you not worked to your greatest potential? It is not easy to make big changes but when you truly focus on your goals, it makes those tough decisions much easier. One of the first steps is to walk away from anyone who is: envious, evil, self-centered, malicious negative, jealous, dysfunctional, unsupportive and unkind. You have a responsibility to your future to eliminate those who are draining your resources. It is not a selfish or narcissistic move, it is in the name of self-love, self-care and in the best interest of your health, well-being and future.

As you move toward your dreams, you will find that on the path of pursuit you will be changed in so many unimaginable ways. You have to be open to the old falling away and the new gravitating into your circle. You will become such a powerful strong, dedicated person that you will begin to engage the world with such confidence and calculation that many unconceivable opportunities will simultaneously arise to meet you on your path. Once you begin to become aware of "who you ARE", you will realize that you are a being of unlimited determination and power.

"Live as if you were to die tomorrow. Learn as if you were to live forever."

Mahatma Gandhi

A common term used in business is ROI: Return on Investment. In any business endeavor it does not makes sense to invest unless there is a return on your investment. Profit is the goal of any business venture. Another way to look at your life is through the lens of economics. I suggest to all of my students to take both economics and business law, which will help you to understand how the world works. If you want to receive dividends then you have to invest wisely. If you wish to reach your goals then you have to INVEST IN YOU!

Jim Rohn, asserted that even if you must work for someone, while you are earning that (limited) income, you can always find ways to simultaneously work on YOU. While you are working, always do your BEST at your job (this is not an excuse to not give your ALL); but during that time, you can make personal improvements. While you <u>are</u> working here are some things you can also work on:

- Handshake
- Smile
- Demeanor
- Speech
- Knowledge
- Skillset
- Intensity
- Desire
- Vision
- Goals

Every job I held in my life kept that fire of desire burning. Each position inspired me to push to learn, grow and evolve. The driving force for me was the consideration that if I ceased to push that I might be stuck at that job forever. Transformative thinking is crucial. Know that you have more inside of you than you perceive. There are gifts that you have not accessed yet. What you need to do is become the best version of yourself, while following your heart. Challenge yourself. Push yourself. Maximize every minute you are given.

You are a product of your thoughts. You are a product of your words. You are a product of how you use your time. Find time during the course of your day to think about what you could do to maximize the time you have. One example, if you want to begin learning a foreign language, use your fifteen-minute break on your job to learn a few words or phrases. Over the course of a year, you can become better than a beginner at anything with a small focused investment of time. The bonus is that you are actually getting paid to do it because you are on the work clock. Invest your time in all ways that will benefit you. Say yes to whatever it takes every day that adds to your value. Be imaginative. Be creative. Be resourceful. Make an effort to find something to do every single day that will enhance your resume.

"There is nothing impossible to him who will try."

Alexander the Great

Once you start to see a world of possibility, nothing is impossible. Success is not certain but I know that certain spiritual death occurs in those who do not pursue greatness. Do you see the impossible? I never see impossible; I see it always as: **I'm possible**. Anything is possible. Everything around you was once an imagined item in someone's mind that was brought to reality. In life the opportunities you have are typically disguised as inconvenience, problems, challenges, opposition and doubt. Most people will resign when the path is difficult. My mentor, Maurice Richter said something to me when I was twenty years old that I never forgot:

"Opportunities typically come at inopportune times."

The challenges are NEVER more than you can handle. The challenges are ever present. The challenges are in place to illustrate whether or NOT you REALLY want what is on the other side. In my life, I have learned first-hand that the biggest adversary is our belief. A common belief is that there is a RIGHT TIME to do something; so, we wait for the RIGHT TIME. **STOP DOING THIS.** The truth is: you will never find the convenient time to jump off the cliff towards your destiny. You will never find a convenient time to get married and start a family. You will never find a convenient time to study for exams. You will never find a convenient time to clean your house. You will never find a convenient time to work out. The power to create is yours but you will have to be willing to <u>make the time</u>. You will never find a convenient time to blaze the trails of the unknown. However, if you do not make the attempt, you will most certainly, one-hundred percent FAIL.

> **"Difficulties strengthen the mind, as labor does the body."**
>
> **Seneca**

Lucius Annaeus Seneca urges your focus to be on the benefits attributed to the challenges of existence. To face adversity allows you to build the mental fortitude to rise amidst the challenges of life. To live life is to embrace the difficulties and learn to learn everything you can through the experiences. Forget about simple inconveniences, during this life you will be faced with death, loss, anguish, and excruciating suffering and pain. You need to not only be able to face these hardships, but to work through them. You need to learn to work through tears. You need to learn to work through depression. You need to work through anger. You need to prove to yourself what you are truly made of. As a professor, my students will miss deadlines and come to my office with a variety of excuses. I will never forget the one student who stood across from me in my office and was there to tell me that her brother had been murdered. I couldn't believe it. I stood in reverent awe how she not only prioritized her education but that she knew it was the best thing she could do for her emotional well-being. The successful all have stories of rising above the challenges of their goals and simultaneously the difficulties of LIFE.

The successful have all learned to thrive on these circumstances because they know that it is going to make them tougher, stronger and more resilient. In my experience, when there was a goal on the other side of that chasm it is ALWAYS worth it. I mentioned earlier the story of JK Rowling and how she overcame numerous rejections until finally finding a publisher for the Harry Potter series. As well, she epitomizes the ability to continue onward despite what life throws at you.

This is also part of J.K. Rowling's story: At age 17, she was rejected from college. At age 25, her mother died from disease. At age 26, she suffered a miscarriage. At age 27, she got married. It was a rocky and tumultuous marriage riddled with challenges, despite those her daughter was born. At age 28, she got divorced and was diagnosed with severe depression. At age 29, she was a single mother living on welfare. At age 30, she didn't want to be on this earth. But, she directed all her passion into doing the one thing she could do better than anyone else. And that was writing. At age 31, she finally published her first book. At age 35, she had released 4 books, and was named Author of the Year. At age 42, she sold 11 million copies of her new book, on the first day of release. Remember how she considered suicide at age 30? Today, Harry Potter is a global brand worth more than $15 billion dollars. Never give up. Believe in yourself. Be passionate. Work hard. It's never too late.

Les Brown considers any loss or challenge as an investment for your future. Life is HARD, you need to power through, persevere and know, YOUR life is always YOUR responsibility. Choose your hard. You have to be willing to face disappointment. You have to be willing to face doubt. You have to be willing to face rejection. You have to be willing to face failure. Commit and refuse to stop until you succeed. No one is going to help you and as I am writing these very words, I am exhausted; but when would the book get written? My heart is shattered in a thousand pieces but staying in bed is not going to complete the manuscript. In the words of John C. Maxwell: "Dreams don't work unless you do." Stand up, stand tall and stand firm for your best life.

NEVER SETTLE!

"Success by the yard is hard, but success by the inch is a cinch."

Jim Rohn

It is virtually impossible, sans winning the lottery, to go from nothing and then overnight to the dream life. Solid work over time is required because success cumulative. Essential skills and wisdom are accumulated over time. While winning the lottery sounds enticing, do you possess the understanding to handle the responsibilities that ensue after such a windfall. Make this the last day you will allow your adversities to stand in your way. Start today with small wins and those will eventually grow into the big wins. Step by step, piece by piece you will expand outward, upward and towards your goals. Far from perfect will ever be the conditions and situations in life but realize you will never know how things will turn out; typically, it is better than you could have imagined. The secret: continuously move forward and then things will start to make sense. Do not rush the process. Trust the process. Do not question what is. Trust the what is. Do not look at others. Trust in your *own* story. Do not worry about each footstep. Trust that with each step in the right direction it will all unfold in time. Do not fixate on the present location. Trust that the destination will be more beautiful than you could have ever imagined.

"One day, in retrospect, the years of struggle will strike you as the most beautiful."

Sigmund Freud

Most success stories include humble beginnings, toils of work, burdens of struggle and sacrifice to get to their noteworthy positions. Let's return to the iceberg analogy. Take a moment in your journal to draw an iceberg and meditate that what we see on the surface is only about ten percent of its entire mass. Below the visible tip of my iceberg as a professor is a complete immersion in graduate school from age twenty-two to thirty-two. During that pivotal ten-year period, I simultaneously held down two non-academic jobs, multiple adjunct teaching positions and various research assistant positions. I worked six to seven days a week; never slept until the work was done. Before you wish you had what others have, you have to ask yourself the question: Am I willing to do what they have done? You need to carefully evaluate what others have done before you, you will discover that for every success story there is an incredible invisible iceberg. The lesson is to put in the deep foundational work from the start. If you do not learn to mindfully delay gratification and have a laser focus on your growth and goals you will likely not achieve them. Delay is always part of the design. Delay does not mean denial. Delay means that you are willing to wait until you can enjoy the fruits of your labor. There is no success without sacrifice and you and you alone have to decide how bad you want to achieve your goals. It is you and only you that can decide what are you willing to sacrifice in the process towards progress.

Remember how strong you are as you navigate into the unknown. Continuously revamp your character, continuously improve but NOT until you achieve your goal BUT through the finish line; you cannot STOP. Once you push through that goal the work continues. Once you reach the destination, enjoy the view and do celebrate. BUT at that moment it is time to re-view, re-evaluate, re-assess and prepare for the next race. Moreover, success is about maintaining what you have attained because life does not cease once you get the medal. The successful always continue onward and upward because we know no other way to exist.

Listen to Spiritual, Motivational and Positive messages every day!!!

You set the example every single day of your life. Every day you have to keep doing it. Make today count. Step up, step forward and get after it.

Success is traversing the desert. Success is cutting a trail through the jungle. Success is climbing Mount Everest. All of these tasks share a common principal: you can only accomplish them by taking one-step at a time. Success is finding the Zen in each of those steps. I decided many years ago that I would always shovel my driveway in the winter. I do have a snowblower but I choose NOT to use it; I use the experience as a moving meditation. It serves as a reminder that anything that is seemingly insurmountable can be accomplished with steady, focused and deliberate action. The snow <u>will never</u> and <u>can never</u> defeat me because no matter how much snow is dumped on my driveway, I can clear it, one-shovel at a time. No matter how heavy it snows, no matter how long it snows, it will not snow forever and after the work is done, I can rest, recharge and get back out and shovel again. Any task can be accomplished if you approach it with the appropriate mindset, dedication, energy, fire, bravery and tools; it can be done and it will be done!

The bigger the dream, the harder the climb. I was an athlete. I was at the start of my career one of the most unathletic athletes to grace the field. However, I decided that it was going to be my mission in high school to be the best. I did <u>my best</u> but I was never <u>the best</u>. I was not <u>the best</u> football player. I was not <u>the best</u> wrestler. I was not "the best" lacrosse player. But I was <u>the best</u> I could be. I gave it my all in every way possible. I gave my all at practice. I gave my all off the field training. For me, for three consecutive years there was no off-season. I was taught to fight from whistle to whistle. I did not stop until the contest was over and I knew in my heart that all I had was left on the field. I took those lessons with me beyond the games. If you want to be <u>the best</u> you cannot negotiate with yourself. You need to decide and stick with the plan; decide the work is non-negotiable.

Success always leaves clues along the way. As you proceed towards your destiny you need to maximize your progress daily. Take more deliberate action, while using all your available senses to advance, keep your eyes open and follow the divine breadcrumbs. Avoid at all costs the dream killers: procrastination and excuses.

> **"You can hide memories, but you can't erase the history that produced them."**
>
> **Haruki Murakami**

What are you going to do with your past? Past trauma? You can transcend it all. You can take it all and spin that straw into gold. Two individuals can have the same thing happen to them but have different results. Even more telling, the fact that two siblings can have the same difficult childhood and one becomes successful and the other fails in life. Why? …because one through their history finds drive and the other finds blame. It is a choice!

Affirmations, yoga, mantra, religion, therapy, running, etc. are all techniques that you can utilize to tap into your deepest sense of self. However, any technique is useless without full and complete open-hearted vulnerability, surrender, acknowledgement and acceptance of you (and your past). In order to "do" you must be able to "be". You must be-come incontrovertibly moved by the words you speak and the actions you take. The person who truly moves from their heart be-comes a magnet for miracles.

> **"Blessed is she who believed, for there will be a fulfillment of those things which were told her from the Lord."**
>
> **Luke 1:45 NKJV**

You must take full responsibility of your past choices that have led you to this moment. Accountability is essential. Before this new journey begins, I believe you need to clear the historical and begin anew. There is nothing you can do to change it, so reconcile with your past, find the message in the mess and <u>move on</u>. You do not have to be the same person you were yesterday. We all have transgressed and did things that were aren't proud of. The most important part is that we learn from our history and to not repeat the same mistakes. It is easy to recall the regrets, guilt, remorse, anger, blame and allow it to derail our present moments. We carry those intangible yet heavy memories from the past in our backpack but we need to put them down. As well practiced as I am does not mean that memories do not on occasion take me to a dark cave. What does that mean? It indicates that this part of my past deserves attention. So, visit that place for a moment, sit with those thoughts and try to figure out the reason for the call; then make your exit promptly back to the light. Past focus takes your present time, the most valuable non-renewable resource you have; so don't stay there too long. Know that age does not always bring wisdom, the aged are typically filled with regrets; either experiences they wish they never had or things they wish they did.

> **"The past is gone, the future is not yet here, and if we do not go back to ourselves in the present moment, we cannot be in touch with life."**
>
> **Thich Nhat Hahn**

Thich Nhat Hahn specified, greet your feelings, welcome them, embrace them, love them…and as I typically say: hold them, rock them, tuck them in and put them to bed. To take this lesson one step further, there is a Hawaiian teaching for forgiveness that I often use. It is a fantastic way to find peace, balance and serenity in moments of crisis. If we find ourselves in a social situation that might be going awry, we can use it to help us to defuse volatility and forgive others. For me it is a mantra that I use to bring myself back to the present moment. Situations and unfavorable outcomes will occur in life and what I have learned is that it is most important to go inward and forgive ourself. Yoda would say:

Ho'oponopono is very simple mantra, though it is only four lines, an easy mantra to embody it is not.

I am sorry
Please forgive me
Thank you
I love you

Forgive yourself for not knowing better. Forgive yourself for not treating yourself better. Forgive yourself for the mistakes and transgressions. Forgive yourself for allowing something. Forgive yourself for giving away your power. Forgive yourself for self-inflicted pain. Forgive yourself for suffering longer than you may have needed. Forgive yourself for unhealthy coping mechanisms used to assuage the pain and suffering used to cope with the past. Forgive yourself for not being good to yourself. Forgive yourself for not being your-self. Forgive yourself because sometimes things are out of your control. Forgive yourself because you cannot change the outcome. The burden of anger and resentment are heavy weights to bear.

"Then Peter came to Him and said, "Lord, how often
shall my brother sin against me, and I forgive him?
Up to seven times?" Jesus said to him, "I do not say to
you, up to seven times, but up to seventy times seven."
Matthew 18:21-22 NKJV

To hold on to negative emotions is to drink poison and expect someone else to feel the effects. You may have this toxin in your bloodstream, flowing in your subconscious and not even realize it. As you begin the process of cleaning and clearing the closets of your being, you will start to realize many of your current thoughts and reactive nature can be attributed to the past. Now is the opportunity to unpack, transmute and release the baggage of your past so you can rise to your highest potential. Wounds are heavy painful burdens but if you do not pull the roots of hatred from your being they will drag you down into the dark. Nelson Mandela forgave those whom imprisoned him for eighteen years, if he did not, he would have not become the man he was destined to be. He would have never become the first black head of state in the history of South Africa. You have to face the dark and keep moving forward. Take a moment to imagine spending almost twenty years in prison, laboring in the limestone mines and yet Mandela kept his vision. You too have the keys to release yourself from your self-imposed prison of pain. The antidote is to acknowledge its existence, open your heart, let it go and lift your gaze forward. Wish for <u>all</u> people, even your enemies, even those who hurt you; love, peace and joy.

> **"Only a fool learns from his own mistakes. The wise man learns from the mistakes of others."**
>
> ### Otto von Bismarck

Remember, there is no substitute for the application of knowledge and that is how you develop true wisdom. Read as many books as you can. Listen to as many podcasts as you can. Take as many classes as you can. Get out there and get experience <u>in</u> the world. Find and harness the strength of spirit and prove to yourself that you can transcend, and you will. Reconcile with who you were for who you are now because you did not come this far to only stop here. It doesn't matter what has happened to you, what matters is to persevere and decide that those events do not DEFINE YOU. Nothing you have been through is wasted, EVERYTHING you have been through, EVERYTHING you have learned is important for YOUR journey. Your future is not about what you have lost along the way, but what you have remaining and that is WISDOM, COURAGE, STRENGTH. Use that as fuel for your fire!

GRATITUDE, MEDITATION, PRESENCE AND PEACE

"Thanks be to God for His indescribable gift!"

2 Corinthians 9:15 NKJV

A common thread in the law of attraction literature is to above all venture to be happy. Joy-Joy-Joy. A common fallacy is to think that once you get what you desire that you will magically be happier than you are right now. You will not be happier after you get the job. You will not be happier after you write the book. You will not be happier married than you are as a couple. You will not be happier in a Porsche than a Toyota. You have to find your joy and fulfillment <u>in</u> the present moment. You have to find happiness now as there is no way to happiness; happiness <u>is</u> the way. The wonderful things that happen along the way are to be considered the sprinkles on the ice-cream sundae of your existence. Once you are able to foster a daily sense of P.E.A.C.E., you will be gifted the keys to your dreams.

Positive Energy Activates Constant Elevation

Your practice must begin at the start of every day. Meditate upon waking to: find appreciation and gratitude; it is the only way to battle negativity

141

and discouragement. Hone in on what is meaningful and valuable to you. You have to focus on what is, not what has been or what may be. Get yourself into a general state of thankfulness. Gratitude is a tool that will facilitate your ability to find the serenity in the present moment. Gratitude will help you find the grace that you are exactly where you need to be to get to where you wish to go. Gratitude is an essential tool on the path to success and your overall well-being. The world is your mirror and it will reflect positive feedback when you continuously seek joy and gratitude; this process is imperative when you are amidst challenges. From another angle, once you establish a gratitude practice it will provide you with a forcefield of goodness against anything that may come your way.

> **"Be grateful for what you already have while you pursue your goals. If you aren't grateful for what you already have, what makes you think you would be happy with more."**
>
> **Roy T. Bennett**

Countless studies have confirmed the profoundly positive effects of gratitude on wellness. Giving thanks daily is a way to rewire your brain and supercharge your life in profound ways. Gratitude will actually boost both your mood and your immune system. Robert Emmons and The Greater Good Science Center have conducted extensive research on the benefits of possessing an attitude of gratitude. Generally, gratitude makes you happier and healthier. If you wish to counter negative emotions when they arise, simply shift your focus and appreciate the moment and the world around you; find something positive and beautiful. There is a simplicity and power to this practice: you cannot be both grateful and unhappy at the same time. It is impossible to be bitter, resentful, sad, regretful, fearful or angry when you are in a state of appreciation. Studies have shown that gratitude, appreciation and acts of kindness release the feel-good dopamine which highlights that old adage that it is (literally) better (for your health) to give than to receive.

"A grateful mind is a great mind which eventually attracts to itself great things."

Plato

Want better sleep? Be thankful. Want to be more resilient under stress? Be grateful. The best part of this practice is that it costs <u>zero dollars</u> and the returns on your investment are limitless. An attitude of gratitude and appreciation enhances health, reduces stress, lowers blood pressure, and motivates you to be more mindful of your wellbeing. Studies have shown that grateful people are more likely to take care of their health and report greater happiness.

Sharing is caring, so remember not to keep your gratitude to yourself. Make it a practice to share your good vibes and thanksgiving with others. Grab your journal and take a moment to jot down a few people that you are grateful to have in your life: loved ones, mentors, teachers and friends. Choose one of those people from your list and prepare a hand-written message of appreciation to that special person and send it in the mail (yes REAL MAIL / SNAIL MAIL / STAMPS / ENVELOPES). Research has shown that this pro-social activity is beneficial in so many ways to both the sender and recipient.

Gratitude will change your life. Gratitude will change everything for the better. Start today! Do not wait for the day to be good, **make it good** by doing **your best**. You are never going to be happy until you absolutely learn to love your life. You are never going to get the more you are seeking until you love the what you have now. The data proves that gratitude will make you a miracle magnet. The practice is certainly challenging. However, once you start the process, you will find more and more things to be grateful for in your life. As well, over time it will be easier to get yourself into a state of appreciation. Moreover, the way you perceive even the "negative" things in your life will be brighter. I have practiced to become a silver linings guy: I am always of the perspective that all things are working to my greatest good. I realize the longer that I live, that it all makes complete sense in retrospect. Be thankful, be grateful, be appreciative and find the beauty in the clouds.

143

Gratitude Journal

"Write it on your heart that every day is the best day in the year."

Ralph Waldo Emerson

For the next 21 days, your mission if you choose to accept it, is the daily task of maintaining a gratitude journal. Why? Well, reread the last section again, do some research of your own and also know that this practice actually reduced the blood pressure of participants in one of the studies. Wow!

Don't stress over it! Many people find it challenging to pinpoint exactly what it is that they are grateful for in their lives. Take a deep breath and know there are never any wrong answers and as you practice it will become easier and easier over time. The way I begin is simple, I will look at what is right in front of me: I am grateful for my eyes, my sight and my hands as I type these words on the computer. I am thankful for my fingers, my toes and my breath. I am thankful for the comfy pillows on my bed. I am thankful for the clothes I am wearing and the shoes on my feet. I am thankful for the smile on my child's face. I am thankful for the present company of my beloved right here next to me. Once I get started, once I get the juices flowing, I then continue onward and upward for a minute or two as I begin to be filled by the grace of gratitude.

"Wear gratitude like a cloak and it will feed every corner of your life."

Rumi

Consistent practice will make gratitude an automatic part of your outlook. It will soon become the default way in which you look at situations, your life and the world. Regardless of the amount of time you spend, even just minutes daily; I promise that you will be rewarded. However, to garner the full benefits you need to practice this every day as you are re-training and re-wiring your nervous system to focus on gratitude instead those default foci of lack, frustration, anger, despair, sadness, etc. Nothing comes easy. Nothing happens overnight. Everything worth anything takes time. But it is guaranteed that as you learn to appreciate the world around you and the body you live in, that you will be gifted with even more to be grateful for. As you shift to practice an appreciation mindset, consider this German proverb that is often attributed to Abraham Lincoln: **We can complain because rose bushes have thorns or rejoice because thorn bushes have roses.** Start tomorrow (or even right now) on your twenty-one-consecutive day journey into gratitude.

Day 1 ____/____/_____ I am grateful for

_____

_____

_____

_____

Day 2 ____/____/_____ I am grateful for

_____

_____

_____

_____

Day 3 ____/____/_____ I am grateful for

_____

_____

_____

_____

Day 4 ____/____/_____ I am grateful for

_____

_____

_____

_____

Day 5 _____/_____/_____ I am grateful for

_____

_____

_____

_____

Day 6 _____/_____/_____ I am grateful for

_____

_____

_____

_____

Day 7 _____/_____/_____ I am grateful for

_____

_____

_____

_____

Day 8 _____/_____/_____ I am grateful for

_____

_____

_____

_____

Day 9 _____/_____/_____ I am grateful for

_____

_____

_____

_____

Day 11 _____/_____/_____ I am grateful for

_____

_____

_____

_____

Day 12 _____/_____/_____ I am grateful for

_____

_____

_____

_____

Day 13 _____/_____/_____ I am grateful for

_____

_____

_____

_____

Day 14 _____/_____/_____ I am grateful for

_____

_____

_____

_____

Day 15 _____/_____/_____ I am grateful for

_____

_____

_____

_____

Day 16 _____/_____/_____ I am grateful for

_____

_____

_____

_____

Day 17 _____/_____/_____ I am grateful for

_____

_____

_____

_____

Day 18 ____/____/_____ I am grateful for

_____

_____

_____

_____

Day 19 ____/____/_____ I am grateful for

_____

_____

_____

_____

Day 20 ____/____/_____ I am grateful for

_____

_____

_____

_____

Day 21 ____/____/_____ I am grateful for

_____

_____

_____

_____

"Gratitude, like faith, is a muscle. The more you use it, the stronger it grows."

Alan Cohen

Once you make it to Day 22, take the time to reread all of your entries and consider what you discovered about you in the process? What did you learn about your life? How does it make you feel looking back? Do you feel differently now? How have you grown over the last three weeks? Do you notice any distinct differences in your outlook and perspective? What are you MOST grateful for in this very moment? Over time, it will become clear that you will learn that when appreciation comes first then the blessings of abundance will follow suit much faster. Furthermore, I have learned that true wealth is not money and material objects as most in Western culture believe. True wealth is real-friendship, real-love, self-love, gratitude and peace. As Michael Franti says: **"The best things in life aren't things."**

> **"Therefore I say to you, whatever things you ask when you pray, believe that you receive them, and you will have them."**
>
> **Mark 11:24 NKJV**

What you believe deep inside yourself will manifest in your reality. I wish for you to believe in the power of your belief. You can have whatever you want but it is also a daily practice to keep the blessings that are bestowed upon you. Ancient Hebrew culture had a belief "ever the same in my inmost being: eternal, whole, indivisible, timeless, shapeless and ageless".

Jim Rohn and I urge you to:

- Believe in yourself
- Believe in GOD
- Believe in the community
- Believe in the economy
- Believe that tomorrow can be better than today

God is in you. You are the living spirit. Claim your power and stop condemning yourself. Be grateful. Be grace-full. Be faith-full. You have the choice to disintegrate your limitations. However, most people spend a lot of time denying themselves through their negative self-talk and beliefs. Begin a ritual practice to change those habits to become the new person you wish to be. Paul in the bible discusses the notion of daily death:

> **"I affirm, by the boasting in you which I have in Christ Jesus our Lord, I die daily."**
>
> **1 Corinthians 15:31 NKJV**

"I die daily." What does that mean? Every day we have another opportunity to get it right. Think not about the why you cannot but maintain your focus on the ideal and I promise you that the answers will arrive and the road will rise to meet you.

"For as he thinks in his heart, so is he."

Proverbs 27:3 NKJV

What is really different about the successful and the others? No one knows! What I do know is that it is all a choice. You can choose to believe or not. We make decisions every moment of every day. The hours prior to my writing this particular sentence, my life was rife with scattered energy and procrastination almost won. However, I made the decision to get up, turn on the computer, listen to a podcast and continue to work on this book. You, one day will reach a point in your life that your internal driving force does not allow you to waste a single moment. You, one day will reach a point in your awareness that the call of the future is so loud that it does not allow even a momentary distraction to interrupt your progress. You, one day will reach a point that your future self is constantly reminding you that your time is nigh.

As you move forward towards your goals, forget not to LIVE LIFE. Once you learn to play the game, you will eventually get ahead of the clock. It will become your divine rhythmic metronome and you will be able to use its ticks as blessed inspiration. It is probably why I admire high-quality mechanical watches. Its movement is an acknowledgement of life, like your heartbeat it reminds you that you are still here and you have time; that you can still attain your purpose. You will reach a point when you will begin to feel the power of your position. You will reach a moment when the goodness and grace of life will flow abundantly towards you and over you like majestic waterfalls of abundance. You will reach a point when you will be able to LIVE fully each day and enjoy every marvelous moment.

Mark Twain said: "Sing like no one's listening, love like you've never been hurt, dance like nobody's watching, and live like its heaven on earth". It is not the goal to pursue happiness but to pursue things that are deeply meaningful to you. Joy is fleeting and life will always present difficulties. The goal is to stay grounded and focus on the future so you will quickly recover and prevail. Resilience will become second-nature. Happiness is to be able to do what you love. Happiness is being someone you love. Happiness is being with someone you love. Happiness is having dreams. Happiness is pursuing dreams. Happiness is attaining your dreams.

Flow into each day with appreciation, love and goodwill. Be thankful. Daily affirmations are another great practice to connect with spirit and to ground you in divinity. Scripture says that we will eat the fruit of our words. You are who you are today because of what you have been speaking into and over your life. Each day it is important to consistently plant the seeds of your glory, triumph and success. Recall the power of the subconscious discussed earlier. Recall its power to pull you toward whatever it is that lies beneath the surface of your conscious thought. It is now time for you to enhance your ability to deliberately program and hack your subconscious mind to facilitate the manifestation of your best life.

"Death and life are in the power of the tongue, And those who love it will eat its fruit."

Proverbs 18:21 NKJV

You must make an active decision to replace negative habits and thoughts with positive ones. How much time do you waste on useless scrolling and other trivial tasks? How much do you derail your own progress with doubt and negative thinking? The objective is to create new pathways of thought and habits until they become second nature. We discussed earlier the power of the words that you are speaking out loud. Learn to speak only positive statements over your life every single day. Learn to be careful and deliberate what you say about yourself. Consider how you talk to yourself during the course of a day. For example, if you trip and break something, is your typical self-talk negative or positive? Do you call yourself a bad name? I am so <u>XYZ</u>. I don't want to even write anything that may "get into your head". If you want to shift the course of your life then you must pay close attention to any of these negative default phrases in your programming and begin an immediate process to catch, check, and change them to positive ones.

> **"The greatest obstacle for me has been the voice in my head that I call my obnoxious roommate. I wish someone would invent a tape recorder that we could attach to our brains to record everything we tell ourselves. We would realize how important it is to stop this negative self-talk. It means pushing back against our obnoxious roommate with a dose of wisdom."**
>
> **Arianna Huffington**

I have compiled a comprehensive list of affirmations for you to start your day on the sunny side of the street. This is just a guide, be creative with your own affirmations, you are a genius creator and do whatever gets your juices flowing. As well, there are adjectives that can be used to replace your default XYZ with over time. I heard someone say: speak as if you are speaking to God when you talk about yourself. Always speak life and positivity over yourself. Over time you will begin to FEEL the infinite wisdom and power of the universe flowing to you and through you. Day after day, week after week, month after month and year after year keep speaking it; continuously establish who you are and become it. Check in with your "I AM" before you check your DM, FB, SC, IG or any other SM: social media. Whatever you follow the "I am" with in any statement will pursue you. Learn to stay in control of your words. Learn to stay in control of your day. Learn to take control of your mindset before you let any other potential source influence you. One day you will become unshakeable. One day you will become the influencer. Read through the list aloud and make note which do not feel comfortable to say about yourself. When you read the phrase: I am smart, do you believe it? How often have you spoke against your own intelligence?

Affirmations to Start the Day

I am grateful for this new day

It is a new and wonderful day

I welcome this new day with joy and confidence

I am about to increase in wisdom, stature, and favor with GOD and MAN.

Today is a gift

Today is a joy filled, healthy and harmonious day

I am alive

I am breathing

I am excited for what this day brings

I am present

Today is my day

Today is the best day

Today I am shifting the sails of my life towards my dreams

Today I receive limitless positive energy

Today I am safe

Today I will learn

Today I will grow

Today is an opportunity to learn new things

Today I will have fun

Today I will rise to meet every challenge

Today I will not stop

Today I will be noticed

Today I will have hope

Today I will not give up

Today I will make progress

Today I give and receive unconditional love

I have faith in this day

Today I will recognize the gift of grace

Love, joy and peace will follow me all day long

Today will be filled with love

Today is a beautiful day and there will not be another today

I deserve every opportunity this day offers me

Today will bring new insights and understanding

Today I welcome beauty and beauty welcomes me

Today I feel better than yesterday and worse than tomorrow

Today is the start of a new chapter in my life

I am Affirmations

I am love

I am loved

I am treasured

I love my reflection in the mirror

I allow others to love me

I am divine

I am intuitive

I am beautiful

I am dazzling

I am blessed

I approve of myself

I am favored

I am happy

I am joyous

I am health

I am healthy

I am comfortable in my skin

I am at peace

Today I feel healthy and powerful

I radiate beauty

I am a valuable person

I am relaxed

I am in control at all times

I am satisfied

I am honest

I am productive

I am special

I am worthy

I am worthy of love

I am worthy of abundance

I am worthy of success

I am constantly learning

I am constantly growing

I am motivated

I am full of potential

I am abundance

I am abundant

I am expanding constantly

I am confident

I am prosperity

I am consistently developing

I am prosperous

I am wealth

I am wealthy

I am victorious

Everything is fantastic in this moment

Everything I need arrives at exactly the right time

I am enough

I am whole

I am amazing

I am thriving

I am wise

I am wonderful

I am full of wonder

I am responsible

I am determined

I am focused

I am capable

I am talented

I am phenomenal

I am kind

I am compassionate

I am generous

I am caring

I am cared for

I am a philanthropist

I attract everything I wish for

I love myself

I adore myself

I love my own company

I am patient

I am understood by all

I love everyone, and everyone loves me

I am admired by everyone

I am authentically me

People love to be around me

All of my relationships are in harmony

I am welcome everywhere I go

I am daring

I am powerful

I am authority

I am firmness

I am unbounded

I am limitless

I am infinite

I am disciplined

I am strong

I am supported

I am stable

I am centered

I am balanced

I am courageous

I am poised

I am fearless

I am beautiful

I am full of untapped potential

I am a channel for divine inspiration

I am creative

I am receptive

I am inspiration

I set high goals for myself

I am inspired by the world around me

I am always where I need to be

I am always in the right place at the right time

I am able to deal with any challenges that comes my way with ease

I am capable of overcoming obstacles

I love the struggle

I love the competition

I am a champion

I have the will to win

I am willing to pay the price of success

I am free of the past

I am **not** my past, my past does **not** define me

I am optimistic about my future

It is my time to thrive and shine

I believe in myself

My life is a miracle

I am capable of letting go

I am free to create a new life for myself

I am evolving to my highest potential

I am capable of achieving my dreams

I am consciously choosing empowered thoughts

I am my own best friend

I am my boss

I am the director of my life

I am my biggest cheerleader

I am proud of myself

I am writing the script of my life

I am the master of my destiny

I am excited about my life as it unfolds

I am in the flow of life

I am in the zone

I am creating a most beautiful life

I have the ability to make my life recession proof

Your dreams will never give up on you, it is only you who has the power to give up on your dreams. Motivate YOU and be your OWN cheer squad. Every moment you can return to these three simple affirmations for a quick fix boost:

- I will succeed
- I will thrive
- I will win

"A winner is a dreamer who never gives up."

Nelson Mandela

'What the new year brings to you will depend a great deal on what you bring to the new year."

Vern McLennan

Do not wait for the new year to make resolutions. Start today. Take control of the now and you will have power over your future. It is a new year, a new me AND it starts NOW! Recite these as often as you need. **This is my year**:

...to meet the right people
...to get healthy and whole
...to accomplish dreams
...to go further in my career
...for vindication
...for restoration
...for new beginnings
...to step into a new level of my destiny
**"This bright new year is given me
To live each day with zest
To daily grow and try to be
My highest and my best!"
William Arthur Ward**

"Sleep is a regenerative process where we heal and where our neurons build strong connections. It's like a fountain of youth that we dive into every night."

Mikhail Varshavski

Just as you start your day, it is also important to meditate upon sleep. Spend some time each evening to appreciate the day, its lessons, and its closing. Learn to relax in the knowing that you have no more to do at or in this moment and it is now time to recharge your batteries.

Furthermore, if you are always doing your best, you will always rest easy. You need to learn that your tomorrow has yet to happen and to be excited for the dreams and surprises that await you in the morning. Before bed daily, I typically recite a selection of the above affirmations to myself along with my personal prayers for protection, support and gratitude.

"Even a soul submerged in sleep is hard at work and helps make something of the world"

Heraclitus

As your dreams begin to manifest, you must be made aware that success does not always feel successful. For me, success has always felt lackluster or even melancholic. It may feel strange because you are in a foreign place. Remember, you have never been here before and it may not look as you imagined in your head. As suggested earlier, it isn't as much about the finish line as it is running through it. While I suggest celebrating the victory, remember the fluidity and follow-through that comes with your manifestations.

"His Infernal Majesty leans towards me confidingly. "You have imposter syndrome," He says, "but paradoxically, that's often a sign of competence. Only people who understand their work well enough to be intimidated by it can be terrified by their own ignorance. It's the opposite of Dunning-Kruger syndrome, where the miserably incompetent think they're on top of the job because they don't understand it."

Charles Stross

You have to be strong and stay the course and allow your-self the time to settle into the new you. This period of disorientation is a breeding ground for doubt and it is way more common an experience than people realize. Studies have reported that upwards of eighty percent of people struggle with accepting their achievements and feel as if they do not deserve what they earned. You want to avoid at all costs anything that might hinder this new path of YOU. Your new identity will require just as much work to maintain as it did to acquire it. Doubt was discussed earlier in the book and it is necessary to know that it may never dissipate. The doubt that arises post success is an even deeper cutting uncertainty and if not kept at bay will capsize your boat. Doubt is both a confidence killer and dream destroyer. So, you need to be super vigilant to silence that voice between your ears and behind your eyes.

> **"I still believe that at any time the no-talent police will come and arrest me."**

> **Mike Myers**

In psychology the concept is known as Imposter Syndrome or Imposter Phenomenon. While it is not an officially recognized diagnosis or disorder, it does have two close friends: anxiety and depression. Imposter syndrome is used to describe individuals who are high achieving but simultaneously doubt their own skills and abilities. It is a strong belief that they do not deserve what it was they accomplished. It is thought that the accolade obtained is a product of luck or other external factors.

> Competent people are likely to feel incompetent
> Powerful people are likely to feel weak
> Influential people are likely to feel insignificant
> Intellectual people are likely to feel simpleminded

No one succeeds by chance. No one gets a job accidentally. No one wins an award by coincidence. No one gets a diploma unintentionally. No one gets a promotion by luck. No one gets cast on stage unexpectedly. No one has it ALL together! You have to stave off the negative self-talk that has the potential to derail your success.

> **"I still sometimes feel like a loser kid in high school and I just have to pick myself up and tell myself that I'm a superstar every morning so that I can get through this day and be for my fans what they need for me to be."**

> **Lady Gaga**

The feelings of being a fraud tend to arise most often in those beginning a new endeavor and those who strive for perfection. Regardless of the type of work you will engage, you need to be continuously conscious and self-aware. We all have deficiencies. We all have inadequacies. We all have shortcomings. Not only is it important to know them and consistently improve but **do not** let insecurity take over. It takes practice to push away the: doubt, guilt, anxiety, shame, unworthiness…etc. Many highly successful people walk through their life feeling hopeless; while they have so much to be grateful for. The most blessed people may simultaneously live in a world of despair. You need to believe that your success was the result of hard work. Consistently take time to reflect on your path. Take time to consider the persistence, the late nights, the rejections, the sacrifices, the discipline, the failure, the risks, the efforts…that brought you to where you are. Learn to own what you have earned. Learn to enjoy the life you have built. Learn to pivot when insecurity arises and don't allow it any time to take residence in your beautiful home.

> **"So I have to admit that today, even 12 years after graduation [from Harvard], I'm still insecure about my own worthiness. I have to remind myself today, You are here for a reason. Today, I feel much like I did when I came to Harvard Yard as a freshman in 1999 … I felt like there had been some mistake — that I wasn't smart enough to be in this company and that every time I opened my mouth I would have to prove I wasn't just a dumb actress. … Sometimes your insecurities and your inexperience may lead you to embrace other people's expectations, standards, or values, but you can harness that inexperience to carve out your own path — one that is free of the burden of knowing how things are supposed to be, a path that is defined by its own particular set of reasons."**

Natalie Portman, Harvard Commencement 2015

Awareness is crucial, along with having a strong social network for support during those challenging times. If you do not have someone close, know that even professionals in counseling psychology and psychiatry have their own personal therapists; life is hard for everyone, even the EXPERTS. Just as you have to believe in your dreams, you have to believe that you DESERVE them. You have to believe that you are GREAT. You have to believe that you put in the EFFORT. You have to believe that you put in the TIME. You have to believe that it was <u>your</u> LABOR that brought <u>you</u> to merge with the accomplishments. You have to believe that you have the <u>right</u> to enjoy the fruits of your disciplined life. Here are several mantras to help you to stay above the mire of imposter syndrome:

I am a product of my efforts and abilities
I did not get my job by luck
I am talented, gifted and valued
I am good enough
I do deserve these gifts
I am NOT going to fail

You need to do your best not to deflect or downplay your accomplishments. My personal internal struggle has always been in the area of not being able to fully accept compliments and praise. As a perfectionist, I would know to my core that I had done a great job, but that whispering inner-critic is always focusing on the minutiae of what I did wrong or what I could have done better. While it is not a bad thing to be conscientious, it does keep you somewhat out of the moment and has the potential to impede your progress, especially if it leads to overthinking every decision. I have found that the things that I would hyper fixate on as mistakes, no one even noticed. Remember <u>The Law of Attraction</u>: if you concentrate on your faults, you will become them. Where you focus your attention is what you will attract. What you think is what you will be. So do your best not to contradict the fact that you are a most special individual, that you deserve success and that you are a gift to the world.

Say it out loud: I deserve to live happily ever after!

MOVING FORWARD, PAY IT FORWARD

"Give, and it will be given to you: good measure, pressed down, shaken together, and running over will be put into your bosom. For with the same measure that you use, it will be measured back to you."

Luke 6:38 NKJV

Now that you are truly ready to get firmly on the path, you should take time to consider what you will do with your newly discovered wealth, fame, influence and power. A very important principle to consider is not what you can get from this world, but what contributions will you make to the world and what legacy will you leave behind.

51/49 is an old axiom that has been recently popularized by Gary Vaynerchuk, as much as I love him, his story and his raw presentation style, I do not like to consider the transactional nature that he infuses upon service. If you give with the consideration of what you will get back in return, then it shifts the relationship from service to business. Unabashed in a podcast he pulled back the curtain and detailed this practice. Indeed, it is all true. It is a universal law. It will function in all of the ways he asserts: when you give, you get an increased return…

every-time. However, I do believe in my heart of hearts that the "giver" does not receive the same spiritual return when the giving is done in a transactional manner (for gainful returns); there are greater goals in life than the acquisition of physical currency.

"Life gives to the givers and takes from the takers". Giving is a most selfish act because there is an incredible return on your investment. The gratitude and positive emotions that you receive will elevate you beyond the time and monetary disbursement. The best gifts are the ones that come from the heart.

> **"But this I say: He who sows sparingly will also reap sparingly, and he who sows bountifully will also reap bountifully. So let each one give as he purposes in his heart, not grudgingly or of necessity; for God loves a cheerful giver. And God is able to make all grace abound toward you, that you, always having all sufficiency in all things, may have an abundance for every good work. As it is written: "He has dispersed abroad, He has given to the poor; His righteousness endures forever."**
>
> **2 Corinthians 9:6-9 NKJV**

How much of your-self do you give? How hard do you work? Do you put your all into all that you do? Always try to provide <u>more</u> service than you are paid for, why? Consider what was discussed above and think of it an investment in your future. I have always put all of myself in everything I have ever been tasked to complete. You may not think you are being watched but people are always there observing. You never know who crossed your path while you were flipping pizza dough. You never know who might remember that door you held for them. You never know who saw you perform in the local performance of The Nutcracker. You never know who watched you help that stranger in the grocery store. Take the time to take the extra time to engage your world in the grandest possible way. Consider that extra effort as another way to water the seeds of your future.

"What's Money? A man is a success if he gets up in the morning and goes to bed at night and in between does what he wants to do"

Bob Dylan (Robert Allen Zimmerman)

How do you want to be remembered? What type of letter of recommendation do you want to be provided? The testimony of one customer has the potential to either launch or destroy your reputation. Similar to service, take the time to consider your daily efforts in both time and energy to one day be returned to you three-fold. Never think of what you do not get paid for as a loss. Never consider the time you invested in anything or anyone as a loss. Never consider the love you gave <u>ever</u> as a loss. Instead view everything you have put into the world as an investment to your best and brightest future. One day, all of that love and appreciation will return in the most unexpected and spectacular ways.

An African American proverb posits: Each one, teach one / Each one, help one. As teacher, whether it be academic or yoga, there is no greater gift in the world than to teach a class. Teaching is the most selfishly selfless act. If you can aid or support another human being it will return to you in beautiful warm dividends. Even if you do not yet "know" what your own personal mission and purpose is <u>yet</u>, you can still lend a hand to someone. Giving your time to local organizations will feed your soul. It takes zero effort for one candle to light another.

"Greatness comes through serving. The more you serve, the greater you become."

Edwin Louis Cole

THE END...IS JUST THE BEGINNING

> **"If one advances confidently in the direction of his dreams, and endeavors to live the life which he has imagined, he will meet with a success unexpected in common hours."**
>
> **Henry David Thoreau**

You made it to the end of the book. Now you must advance confidently. Now you must decide to live the life of your dreams. Now you must truly become the author of <u>your</u> book, take the pen and write your own ending. No secrets to success exist. Just as Dorothy learns in The Wizard of Oz, you just have to believe in yourself: "You had the power all along, my dear".

Set your goal.
Understand the obstacles.
Create a positive mental picture.
Clear your mind of doubt.
Embrace the challenge.
Stay on course.
Show the world and yourself you can indeed do it!

I hope you can learn to hear the words in the silence. I hope you can learn to listen to the desires of your heart. I hope you can lift the veils of uncertainty of your mind. I hope you can lift the gates of lack and allow the limitless abundance to flood your life with unceasing happiness and joy.

> **"And you also were included in Christ when you heard the message of truth, the gospel of your salvation. When you believed, you were marked in him with a seal, the promised Holy Spirit, who is a deposit guaranteeing our inheritance until the redemption of those who are God's possession—to the praise of his glory."**
>
> **Ephesians 1:13-14 NIV**

> **"Therefore I will look to the Lord; I will wait for the God of my salvation; My God will hear me."**
>
> **Mikah 7:7 NKJV**

The breeze at dawn has secrets to tell you.
Don't go back to sleep.

You must ask for what you really want.
Don't go back to sleep.

People are going back and forth
across the doorsill
where the two worlds touch.

The door is round and open.
Don't go back to sleep.

"Therefore let us not sleep, as others do, but let us watch and be [a]sober. For those who sleep, sleep at night, and those who get drunk are drunk at night. But let us who are of the day be sober, putting on the breastplate of faith and love, and as a helmet the hope of salvation."

1 Thessalonians 5:6-9

"Use only that which works, and take it from any place you can find it."

Bruce Lee

Lao Tzu expressed in the Tao te Ching that the journey of a thousand miles begins with a single step. Furthermore, there is an Italian Proverb helps to complete Lao Tzu's assertion:

…between saying and doing many a pair of shoes is worn out.

To summate, the trifecta of values for success are: good habits, discipline and commitment. It has been proven that good habits, discipline and commitment are what get things DONE. However, there is one additional super important factor that cannot be prescribed: the unrelenting drive to succeed. Motivation is immeasurable, it is not for sale, it must be harnessed, it must be decided and it can only be personally implemented. I hope that this book has served as the catalyst for that intangible narcotic.

REMEMBER, there are four things that are irreplaceable:

- Time after it is gone
- Opportunity after it is missed
- The word after it is said
- Trust after it is lost

"**If you're going to try, go all the way. There is no other feeling like that. You will be alone with the gods, and the nights will flame with fire. You will ride life straight to perfect laughter. It's the only good fight there is.**"

Charles Bukowski

In closing, I would like to share a phrase that I have heard countless times in the last ten years while writing this book. The exact origin of the saying is unknown but it is commonly attributed to the American boxer Joe Lewis and as well was adopted by the United States Marine Corps:

"**Everyone wants to go to heaven but nobody wants to die.**"
Buckle up your Safety Belt! Get ready and get going!
One Day or Day One?
Either you can or you can't. Either way you are right. You choose.
It is always YOU versus YOU.

"**The first and greatest victory is to conquer yourself; to be conquered by yourself is of all things most shameful and vile.**"

Plato

Anyone who loves themselves to the core will take control of their minutes, hours, days, weeks, months and years. Anyone who values themselves will no longer be the victim of procrastination and self-sabotage. Know that life is and always will be a fantastic rollercoaster taking you to both spectacular heights and gut-wrenching lows. The twists and turns along the way will ALWAYS reveal, if you pay attention, little sparkling affirmations that you are supported, that you are on the right track and that you are safe. The secret is you must BELIEVE, you must TRUST, you must FEAR NOT knowing that you cannot and will not fall off. My wish for you, when that coaster comes to a halt and the ride of your life is over, that you have found all of your dreams but that it was an even better trip than you could have imagined. I hope that it was all worth it and that you feel in the end that nothing was left behind. If you have breath in your lungs, it means your story is NOT OVER!

"Life biggest tragedy is that we get old too soon and wise too late."

Benjamin Franklin

George Bernard Shaw similarly stated that there are three kinds of people: those who make things happen, those who watch what happens, and those who wonder what happened. Go forth, blaze a trail, make things happen and leave your legacy. It is time to stop wondering. It is time to begin visualizing and to start living <u>your</u> dream. As you find your way to your best life, people will wonder if you are a magician and you will not be able to explain all of the intricacies of your personal success story. I know for a fact that once you find your passion, you will reach a point where life becomes your most marvelous dream.

"Life can only be understood backwards; but it must be lived forwards."

Søren Aabye Kierkegaard

When you look back on your life,
When your life flashes before your eyes,
Will you enjoy the show?

"The art of living well and the art of dying well are one in the same"

Epicurus

The inspirational authors, academics, coaches and gurus whom have both influenced me tremendously during my own journey and along the way inspired the creation of this very text.

Aristotle

Marcus Aurelius

Shawn Achor

Richard Alba

James Allen

Chris Bose

Brene Brown

Les Brown

Tom Bilyeu

Peter Bregman

Jack Canfield

Dolores Cannon

Jim Carrey

Kyle Cease

Bobby Chandler

Dave Chappelle

Deepak Chopra

Bikram Choudhury

Thomas Clifford

Alan Cohen

Russell H. Conwell

Ram Dass (Richard Alpert)

Joe DeMeo

Michael Diamond

Lou DiRienzo

Joe Dispenza

W.E.B Du Bois (William Edward Burghardt Du Bois)

Creflo A. Dollar

Wayne W. Dyer

Ralph Waldo Emerson

Robert Emmons (The Greater Good Science Center)

Jerry Flowers

Viktor E. Frankl

Andy Frisella

Robert Fulghum

Steven Furtick

Bill Gates

Khalil Gibran

Malcolm Gladwell

Neville Goddard

David Goggins

Jim Guccione

HAFIZ

Thich Nhat Hahn

Steve Harvey

Stephen Hawking

Louise Hay

Esther Hicks and Jerry Hicks (Abraham)

A.C. Higgins

Napoleon Hill

Adam Horovitz

Ms. Hunter (4th Grade Trinity School)

TD Jakes (Thomas Dexter Jakes)

John K. Jenkins Sr.

Inky Johnson

Matt Kahnwo

Kabir

Helen Keller

Robert Kiyosaki

Bruce Lee

Karyn Loscocco

Nelson Mandela

Marshall Mathers

Abraham Maslow

John C. Maxwell

Gwen Moore

Joseph Murphy

Miyamoto Musashi

Earl Nightingale

Joel Osteen

Lawrence Parker

Prince (Prince Rogers Nelson)

Patanjali

Norman Vincent Peale

Jordan Peterson

Maurice Richter

Mel Robbins

Tony Robbins

Joe Rogan

Jim Rohn (Emanuel James Rohn)

Jalal ad-Din Muhammad Rumi

Reese Satin

Kevin Seaman

Florence Scoville Shinn

John Earl Shoaff

Upton Sinclair

Socrates

Michael Todd

Eric Thomas

Eckhart Tolle

Lao Tsu

Mike Tyson

Robert Matthew Van Winkle

Gary Vaynerchuk

Denzel Washington

Alan Watts

Katt Williams

Jocko Willink

Oprah Winfrey

Dana White

Adam Yauch

Paramahansa Yogananda

Zig Ziglar

CHATGPT

This book was written between the years 2015 and 2024 and some of its origins began in my imagination in the late 1990s. Today we are at the precipice of a new dawn in knowledge production with the advent of robust artificial intelligence. Along with this technological and intellectual growth potential brings about incredible philosophical and existential musings. Just as the previous technological marvels (The Radio, The Television, The Internet) of the past century changed the world, so too will Artificial Intelligence have unpredictable impacts on our lives. We are at a crossroads in the human versus computer relationship. The Internet at its emergence was envisioned as a tool for humanity to grow and evolve in the direction of singularity. Artificial intelligence presents us with a shift in the relationship between the user and the tool. We can not only use this tool but this tool has the potential to direct us in unexplainable ways towards a singularity of intelligence. After being introduced to the technology a year ago, I was very curious as to how AI would have written this book and surprisingly it looks uncannily similar to my ideas, suggestions and writing. Welcome to a new world of knowledge production...

Write three paragraphs on success, setting goals, motivation, determination and satisfaction:

Success is often defined as the achievement of one's goals or desired outcomes. However, success is a subjective and personal experience that can mean different things to different individuals. Setting clear and specific goals is essential for achieving success. Goals provide

direction, focus and motivation to individuals, helping them to move towards what they want to achieve. Moreover, having a plan and a set of goals can help individuals to prioritize their efforts and manage their time and resources more effectively.

Motivation is a crucial element in achieving success. It is the driving force that pushes individuals to take action towards their goals. However, motivation can be fleeting, and it is essential to cultivate it regularly. One way to maintain motivation is to celebrate small wins along the way. Celebrating these small successes provides a sense of accomplishment and fuels the motivation to continue working towards larger goals. Additionally, it is crucial to stay focused on the reasons why one is pursuing a particular goal. Reminding oneself of the benefits and rewards that come with achieving the goal can help maintain motivation and momentum.

Determination is the willpower and persistence to continue working towards a goal, even in the face of challenges and obstacles. Success rarely comes without setbacks and failures, and it is essential to develop a mindset of resilience and determination. It is crucial to learn from failures, adjust one's approach, and keep moving forward. Satisfaction comes from achieving success after overcoming challenges and obstacles. It is the feeling of fulfillment and pride in one's accomplishments. However, satisfaction is not a static state and can quickly turn into complacency. To maintain satisfaction and continue growing, it is essential to set new goals and continue challenging oneself.

Let Us Tell Your Story

by Dr. Roger A. Ramsammy
President, Hudson Valley Community College
Delivered at the College's 69th Commencement Ceremony, May 13, 2023

I wake each morning eager for this WORLD
With the hope to make life warm, NOT COLD
I know someone has already made a sacrifice
It's why I am here... to not let their work be minimized
I don't watch the news
Because sad stories do not brighten my views.
I think not of a negative world
But one that is positive, at least so I am told
I do not try to change what will be
Because there are things that are happening beyond what the eyes can see
Graduates I ask you;
Can you make changes to yesterday?
Or undo anything that you say?

Can you stop the earth from spinning?
Or see the gas you are breathing?

Can you stop tomorrow from coming?
Or hide the sun from shining?

You are here, and if you open your eyes tomorrow!
So live life like it's yours, NOT one that you borrowed!
This is the next step in your journey
So go out there and do your thing **SO WE CAN TELL YOUR STORY**!

Printed in the United States
by Baker & Taylor Publisher Services